FROM MERC

Also by Colin Urquhart

Anything You Ask
Faith for the Future
Holy Fire
In Christ Jesus
Listen and Live
My Dear Child
My Dear Son
My Father is the Gardener
Personal Victory
The Positive Kingdom
Receive Your Healing
The Truth That Sets You Free
When the Spirit Comes
Your Personal Bible

From Mercy to Majesty

Colin Urquhart

Hodder & Stoughton
LONDON SYDNEY AUCKLAND

First published in Great Britain 1995

10 9 8 7 6 5 4 3 2 1

British Library Cataloguing in Publication Data
A record for this book is available from the British Library

ISBN 0 340 64208 4

Typeset by Hewer Text Composition Services, Edinburgh
Printed and bound in Great Britain by
Cox & Wyman, Reading, Berks

Hodder and Stoughton Ltd
A Division of Hodder Headline PLC
338 Euston Road
London NW1 3BH

To
All at Kingdom Faith
who have shared in the whole adventure
of being led by the Lord
'from Mercy to Majesty'

Contents

Thank You

My grateful thanks to those who have helped me with the writing of the book: to Samantha for her many hours at the word processor. To Paula, my assistant, for all her help and encouragement. And, to my dear wife, Caroline, who has loved me through yet another task on top of everything else!

This has been an enjoyable task for me, for I am most thankful to the Lord who in recent months has taught me so much about His mercy, grace, love and majesty – and so has made this book possible. May He use it for His glory.

1

The Mustard Seed

'I have been longing to meet you.' It was the last thing I had expected him to say.

Sitting across the table from me was Hector Gimènez, pastor of a church of over 250,000 in Buenos Aires. Here was a man who had really experienced revival! Nine years previously he had begun evangelising among drug addicts in his city. After only a year he formed those he had reached with the gospel into a church of 500 people. That church has since grown to over a quarter of a million. Why should he want to meet me?

I knew little about Hector. I had been told he was a man who listened to and obeyed the leading of the Holy Spirit; that this was a key factor in the remarkable ministry God had given him. Our meeting took place in Bergen, a beautiful city on the west coast of Norway. It was February 1995 and the city was enhanced in beauty by the snow that had fallen freshly for several days. I had been there for four days preaching and ministering at a conference on Revival and Praise, attended by over 1,000 people from all over Norway and beyond.

The host church, pastored by Enevald Flåten, had begun three years previously, about the same time as Kingdom Faith Church in West Sussex, and had grown to a similar size of about 1,000 worshippers, unusually quick growth for Europe, but no match for the South American revival!

There were remarkable similarities between the two churches. Both had experienced a strong move of the Holy

Spirit since their inception. Both had a national calling and vision, believing that God was going to use them as a catalyst for revival. Both were churches living in a dynamic of faith, with prayer for national revival high on the agenda. And both happened to be facing major building programmes because of the rapid expansion of their congregations.

During the first three days of the conference the Holy Spirit had moved powerfully. On the first day there was a great outpouring of God's joy. Many were drunk in the Spirit and received a great release from God.

On the second day, many were healed and liberated by the power of God. On the third day the Holy Spirit gave us a great revelation of the majesty and glory of God in our worship. Yet there was a sense that, mighty though those three days were, He was going to do something mightier still during the next two days through Hector Gimènez's ministry.

On the fourth day, the Saturday, I had just finished speaking at my last teaching session and was having a quiet cup of coffee in the pastor's office when Hector arrived. He had just flown from the south of Norway where he had spoken on the previous day, and was due to speak at his first teaching session about ten minutes later.

'Oh, really!' That was all I could think of saying, I was so surprised that he would have wanted to meet me. When he told me why, I was even more amazed.

He spoke in Spanish, was interpreted into Norwegian, and my interpreter then translated for me into English. This cumbersome mode of communication did not lessen the impact of what he was saying.

'A few days ago,' Hector began, 'I was sitting in my hotel room and turned on the television. You were ministering at a meeting. I could not understand your English or the translation, so I had no idea what you were saying. But I could see the power of the anointing that was on you. I said to the Lord, "I want to meet that man." The Holy Spirit told me that I would meet you soon and that when I did so, I would pray for you and impart something from Him to you, and you would impart something to me.'

I was stunned by what Hector said. There was no time to tell him that, while praying during the previous night, the Lord had told me that He would use him to impart something of great significance to me. Hector then took the wind completely out of my sails.

'I want you to come and preach in my church in Buenos Aires. We are opening a new building in August and I want you to speak at some of the special meetings we are holding then.'

The whole conversation was the complete reverse from what I had anticipated. It was I who had been looking forward to meeting Hector. Instead of returning to England after my speaking commitments I had chosen to stay on in Bergen so that I could sit under his ministry. I needed him to come to our church. It was I who wanted to invite him to come to England, for clearly the man must be able to bless our nation with his anointing.

Again I was only able to mumble a response in surprise before Hector was summoned to speak at the conference session.

As I listened to him tell of the events that led to the beginning and subsequent amazing growth of his church, I could not help wondering what God was going to do in me. I had a sense that something of great moment was about to happen, that the Lord was preparing me for something truly significant. I had certainly functioned under anointing in the early part of the conference; and yet I could see in this man an anointing beyond anything I had myself. I had led the people to the limit of my anointing. I soon saw that he was able to take them on still further.

At the end of one of the teaching sessions the Lord spoke clearly to me, saying that I already had what I had been praying for! I had experienced revival previously in my life and ministry and knew we were very close to revival at the Kingdom Faith base at Roffey Place. The Lord explained to me that He had never withdrawn the anointing that I had known at such times. He was going to release that anointing afresh, but He was also going to add a dimension of anointing I had never had before.

During the time of prayer at the end of one of Hector's talks, I had a vision of the heavens being opened and many angels descending. It seemed that God was about to do something mighty. And He did – at the evening meeting!

Hector preached another anointed message and at the end surprised me yet again by telling everyone about the television programme he had seen in his hotel room, this time elaborating on his conversation with the Lord from the brief summary he had given me that morning. He then asked me to come forward.

He asked if I was familiar with mustard seeds and told me that he wanted to use them symbolically. As I held out my hand, he poured into it some mustard seeds.

He then began to speak and prophesy over me. At the time it was difficult to take in all that he was saying. He was standing immediately in front of me, holding my hands in his and speaking in Spanish. Immediately to the right of me was his interpreter translating into Norwegian for the benefit of all present. On my left was my interpreter speaking the English translation into my ear. And I was trying to concentrate on Jesus!

A few days later my younger daughter, who speaks fluent Spanish, translated from the videotape exactly what was said:

> I want to put this mustard seed in your hands. The other night at the hotel I was watching the television. The Lord told me that I was going to meet you and that I must share with you the blessing God gave me. And that God wanted to entrust a key to you . . . to entrust you with the keys for your city, for your country. But you are going to travel through the world and you are going to impart this anointing to many.

Symbolically, I put this mustard seed in your hands. I pray for you, pastor. I put a fresh anointing in your hands and so the Lord says:

> You have sown with tears but the time has come in which you will harvest with shouts of great joy. Abundance. Multiplication that has never been seen in your land. It will be seen and *your* eyes will see it. *You* are included in this.
>
> And tonight I have put a reproductive seed into your hands, something supernatural, a supernatural growth; fresh anointing for your city,
> for your church,
> for your land,
> for where the Lord sends you.

At this point Hector looked straight into my eyes with such love. With great graciousness he then said: 'Humbly, pastor, what God has given me I impart to you. Receive. Be filled. Receive. It's something fresh, something new. Here it is. Here it is. Jesus . . .'

At that point the Holy Spirit came on me so powerfully that I fell to the floor. For several minutes I lay there deeply conscious of the Lord's presence and knowing that something awesome was happening to me.

On the video-film I saw that while I was on the floor Hector addressed all those present, saying to them, 'There's a powerful anointing here. There's a powerful anointing here. Pastor Colin is overflowing. Pastor Colin is overflowing. And when a cup overflows, it splashes on all that surrounds it. We are overflowing here now. Receive what God is anointing, imparting here. Receive. Receive. Receive. Receive what is overflowing. God is giving. Receive. Receive. Receive.'

At that point the Holy Spirit fell on the whole meeting. The glory of God was upon His people. For nearly one and a half hours there followed a time of glorious, exuberant praise for

God. There was such release among the people. 'Where the Spirit of God is, there is liberty.'

After several minutes flat on my back on the floor, I joined in this tremendous time of worship. There was no time to evaluate what had happened to me, and I only had a sketchy idea of what exactly had been prayed over me. But I knew for certain that God had imparted something very powerful to me.

Although it was about 11.30 p.m. by the time the meeting ended, the speakers and leaders were scheduled to have supper together. As I sat at the table I was stunned by the events that had taken place; and yet the Lord had more surprises in store for me.

For over twenty minutes Hector did not appear for the supper. When he finally entered the room he was very excited. He sat opposite me and explained to all present: 'The Lord told me that as I travelled the world, every now and again He would ask me to pray for someone in the way I prayed for Colin this evening. He promised that when I did so He would bless both me and my church.'

He then addressed me: 'When you were on the floor, I saw an exceedingly bright shaft of light come from heaven and fall on you. It was so bright that it reflected off you and on to me. As it did so I received fresh anointing from God. Yes, I received a fresh anointing tonight. The anointing on you was so powerful that it also overflowed to all the people.' Hence the words he had spoken to them while I was on the floor.

Hector continued: 'I was so excited that I felt I should phone my church in Buenos Aires. They told me that something wonderful is happening there. The glory of God has fallen on the people and they cannot stop the meeting. There are so many miracles and wonderful things happening, they cannot stop the meeting. I asked when exactly the Spirit fell upon everyone; and it was at precisely the same time that I prayed for you here!'

I was awestruck. What was it that God had said to Hector when he watched the television programme? That he would impart something to me and I to him. I had wondered what I could possibly impart to him. Now, it seems, he had also received a fresh anointing – and I had been used to impart this to him while I was flat out on the floor!

What an evening! I hardly knew what to think as I returned to my hotel.

On the following morning, Hector ministered to the pastors and leaders. Even though everyone caught the overflow, I had been somewhat self-conscious of the fact that the previous evening's ministry had centred on the anointing God had imparted to me. I still did not know all that had been prayed over me, but for several days felt the power of the Spirit overwhelming me again and again, sometimes at the most unlikely moments.

One thing was clear to me. God had brought me to an entirely new place of anointing and I was to pray for others that they too should receive fresh anointing from Him. The mustard seeds represented the anointing for miraculous multiplication that would enable people to produce abundant fruit in their lives and for churches to grow speedily in revival.

When I returned to England, I knew that I had to share this anointing with everyone in Kingdom Faith. For three years we had been moving into a greater dynamic of revival. I knew that this was the anointing we needed to move us into the release of God's power for which we had been longing.

Already the Holy Spirit had moved upon us in a succession of ways. We had experienced a revival in prayer, in worship, in faith, in love and in the release of joy. Now something of another order had taken place in me, and I knew this would need to be shared by all on the ministry team of Kingdom Faith, together with the students from our Bible College.

There are about sixty-five people on the team of Kingdom Faith Ministries. We meet together with our ninety-five Bible College students every weekday morning at 8.00 a.m. On the Tuesday morning, I shared with everyone what had taken place in Bergen.

In common with many others, I had marvelled for years at the amazing growth of churches in Korea, in parts of West Africa and in South America. A few churches in the hundreds of thousands, several churches with congregations of tens of thousands, and most were only a few years old. What could account for this phenomenal growth?

Some have pointed to the cell group system in Korea, or have used the excuse that there are great cultural differences between Asia, Africa, South America and Europe. This is true but it would be almost blasphemous to suggest that the Holy Spirit could only work in such ways in certain cultures. He is not limited by culture. He is God.

Cell groups have been a system used in some churches to express revival and enable growth; but they have not been the cause of this phenomenal growth. Many churches have tried to imitate the system, but with nothing like the same success, not because of differences in culture but in anointing.

Listening to Hector Gimènez, it was apparent that it was this seed for miraculous multiplication that was present in those areas. **Without that particular anointing there would not be the same fruit or success in other areas, no matter what method of church growth was employed.**

Yes, it was all a matter of anointing, and then of building around that anointing. God had now graciously imparted to me an anointing far beyond anything I had previously known.

Somehow I knew this, although I had yet to see the outworking of that anointing. I needed to pass this anointing on to others, although this did not mean that I was to pass on my anointing to others. Hector had been told to pass on his anointing to me because that was the order of the anointing I needed to fulfil the national and international ministry to which God has called me. Not everyone in Kingdom Faith Ministries has that calling. God anoints us for the fulfilment of what He calls us to do in His Name.

However, it was obvious that every believer in Hector's

church in Buenos Aires had this anointing for multiple growth – that is why the church had grown in such a phenomenal way.

God always builds around anointing. Obviously Hector's anointing was at the heart of the work there. But this does not mean the move of God was dependent on one man. His responsibility was to impart anointing to the whole body, so that the entire congregation could be part of this rapid reproductive process.

And so it would be with us. I needed to see this 'mustard seed' planted in each member of our team, in every student and then, on the following Sunday, in every member of Kingdom Faith Church.

As people listened on that Tuesday morning there was a sense of awe in what God was saying to us, mixed with a keen sense of expectation. There is great openness to God among us and I knew that everyone would want to receive what God was willing to impart.

When I began to pray with people, they immediately fell to the floor under the power of God – and stayed there for some considerable time. The Lord was obviously doing a deep work, planting this seed deeply within people, so that in due course rivers of living water would pour out of them in abundance.

Soon the entire floor of our worship hall was filled with prostrate bodies, and others had to wait until there was room before I could pray for them.

This was very different from the scenes of spiritual drunkenness and exuberant joy that were common when we experienced the refreshing of the Holy Spirit some months previously. This was of another order. There was a deep sense of peace and an awesome sense of God's presence. Nothing particularly dramatic seemed to be taking place, but there could be no doubt that God was imparting something of great significance.

Not all were able to describe precisely what God had done, although they were aware that a deep work of the Spirit had taken place in them. Some knew they had experienced an encounter with God beyond anything they had known previously. But we were not looking for experiences as such. The planting of seed could not be described as 'exciting'. What matters is the fruit that results from the planting.

On Sunday I was supposed to leave for a leaders' conference in Germany, but knew I should delay my departure for a day so that I could pray with all the church members on Sunday morning. Both services were full and at both the same scene was repeated; the floor of the worship hall was filled with prostrate bodies and there was a deep sense of the Lord's presence.

I knew the seed had been planted and that at the evening service I should begin watering it with God's Word. I preached on Jesus's victory, but never finished the sermon. Spontaneously, while I was still preaching, people stood up and praised God. The glory of God had fallen upon His people. It was like a repetition of the great release of anointing that had taken place in Bergen on the evening Hector Gimènez prayed for me.

At last the breakthrough had come. After three years of seeking God and moving progressively towards this point we were now in revival! Yes, I knew we were in a new place with God and that from that moment everything would be different in Kingdom Faith Church and in the entire ministry. Now we could see the fulfilment of everything God had promised us and of the many prophetic words spoken over this ministry by several of His servants from many parts of the world.

Most important of all, God had planted in this nation the seed of revival that could produce the phenomenal growth in the Church that other nations had experienced.

We could not afford to be proud or complacent, for the anointing had to be translated into fruitfulness. We would need to move out as His witnesses in the world. Without the anointing, though, we could not see a move of God that could transform the spiritual state of our land and overflow to several other nations.

This book tells of the events that led up to this time. It will concentrate especially on the things the Lord taught us from His Word, and some of the things He did in our corporate life to prepare us for this time.

Above all it must be realised, as David Yonggi Cho constantly affirms, that these events were God's answer to what is always at the heart of revival: PRAYER.

2

The Tip of the Arrow

You may wonder by now why God should have decided to give such an anointing to me of all people. The answer is simple. It is a work of His mercy and grace!

I could not imagine anybody more unworthy, or even unsuitable, for such a privilege. However, none of us can escape God's call and purpose for our lives, even if we want to. And there had certainly been times, especially in the past year, when I had wanted to escape from the implications of things God had said to me, both directly and through others.

A number of people had publicly prophesied over me during recent years, each using the same description, without knowing that others had brought a similar message. The same prophetic word through several different witnesses, men of international repute.

They said I was like the tip of the arrow breaking through into revival. The Lord had aimed and fired this arrow; so it would inevitably land on target. It was encouraging to recall this during the years of praying for revival in the nation.

Wherever the tip penetrated the rest of the arrow would follow. Every time I heard this part of the prophesy it made me aware of the awesome responsibility God seemed to be giving me. I knew there was no escape! I was sure, though, that only by His grace could I possibly fulfil what He was asking of me.

In 1990 the Lord gave me a word for this decade. He

promised we would see 'five years of steady growth, followed by five years of phenomenal blessing'.

In 1989 we had virtually a new start to the ministry. From the dozen I then had on the ministry team, we had grown to nearly a hundred on the full-time staff of Kingdom Faith. In addition to Roffey Place, our main base in West Sussex, three other bases had opened in different parts of England.

In 1992 the new church was started and by the beginning of 1995 had grown to approximately a thousand. In addition we had lost count of the hundreds of groups all over the nation that were using *The Way of the Spirit Teaching Course*, the Bible teaching course produced and used at Roffey Place, and nearly twenty other teaching centres had been established in various parts of the country to service these.

If this was steady growth, what would the time of phenomenal blessing bring?

The first year of the promised time of great blessing was 1995. I knew the Lord would have to do something significant in me personally, and in the Body corporately, for this to become reality.

Someone with an internationally respected prophetic ministry had given me this word: 'You have seen the thirty-fold and the sixty-fold in your ministry; now you are going to see the hundred-fold. The difference between the sixty and the hundred-fold is that you will do less, but you will see the Lord do more!'

I was trying to come to terms with what the Lord was doing in me through my encounter with Hector Gimènez and realised that our ministry could not enjoy phenomenal blessing without an anointing for phenomenal growth. Only then could we see the outworking of what God had promised.

I was only too conscious that no merit could be attached to me for what God was doing. The only way that I could be ready to receive such a blessing was by knowing that I never could be ready! To impart such an anointing was totally a work of God's grace. Grace is only grace when you do not deserve what God wants to give. If you deserve anything, then what is given is not the work of grace.

In 1992 when the Lord told me to begin Kingdom Faith Church, I had reduced my overseas travelling from about four months in the year to two weeks. Dan Chesney had come to join me in establishing this new congregation. The Lord had impressed on us that this would be the first of a number of new large revival churches He was going to raise up in different parts of the nation. This church was to be a kind of model for other revival churches that would develop. It would be a church of thousands, and would begin with steady growth before experiencing the phenomenal blessing the Lord had promised.

All this sounded very pretentious when we had the inaugural meetings in March of 1992. However, I knew that if I believed what God was saying, I must have the courage to speak the vision into being, even before the new church existed as such.

For such a vision to be fulfilled, this new church would have to begin with a move of God. We decided to have three weeks of inaugural meetings. There would be a service on twenty-two consecutive evenings. However, we announced that before each meeting we would meet together to pray for an hour. Prayer is the key to revival!

We had a core of about thirty-five Bible College students at that time and our team (considerably smaller than it is now) to pray for these meetings. We knew that we had to teach people how to pray, how to engage their hearts with God's heart. How to meet with God in prayer. How to hear from Him and to break through to new places with Him. To learn important principles of spiritual warfare and how to persevere and prevail in prayer.

We would not achieve our objective by speaking about these things, but by showing people by example how to do them; a little teaching followed by practical application.

The Spirit of God began to move powerfully in these prayer meetings, so much so that many people were coming straight from work to be present at them. I saw people running from the car park into the worship hall because they did not want to miss anything God was going to do in the prayer meetings!

Many discovered for the first time in their lives that prayer meetings can and should be exciting, for our God is an exciting God! There is nothing boring about Him. However, these were not the traditional kind of prayer meetings, where people sit around listening to others pray before saying 'Amen'. Everybody was learning how to be fully involved in the prayer.

As we began the three weeks of meetings we were hoping that we would be in revival by the end. We wanted to see a great release of God's power and glory in our midst. By the end of the three weeks we certainly were enjoying a move of God, but could not describe this as full-blooded revival. In April the first group was taken into membership of Kingdom Faith Church: 230 people. That is a fair number with which to begin a church.

However, we could not be complacent in any way. The Lord had told us that this had to be a revival church and so we would need to be moving forward towards this objective. It was to be a church of thousands; 230 was only a start!

At the end of the initial meetings people were tired. It had been a very intensive time. We recognised that it would not be possible to maintain the same degree of intensity without causing exhaustion. We decided to keep the emphasis on prayer, having open prayer meetings before the services on both Sunday mornings and evenings. Every few months we would have another revival week: eight evenings of meetings. We would intensify the prayer in preparation for these, especially with the members of the Kingdom Faith team and the students from the Bible College.

Our expectation was that during each of these revival weeks, God would take the whole church to an entirely new place with Him, releasing more of the dynamic of revival among us.

This certainly happened. As each revival week approached we continued to expect that the final breakthrough into revival would happen. Although this did not take place, God blessed us richly, sorted many things out in our lives, and released His Holy Spirit in fresh anointing upon us.

The faith of the congregation continued to grow. Our great strength was that every member was committed to the concept of revival. We were becoming a praying people, and constantly held the vision of the church before everyone. If they were not committed to the vision, then they were in the wrong place. The vision was simple:

A people living in the revival power of Jesus Christ their Lord:
Committed to the life of faith in God's Word;
Laying down their lives one for another in love;
And revealing His light and truth to the world.

Every revival week brought further fulfilment of this vision in our lives and led to further growth in the church. In the following chapters, I will trace the way the Lord led us through His Word, preparing for the anointing that has now brought us into the time of phenomenal blessing.

The Holy Spirit is the Spirit of Truth and guides us into the truth of God's Word. Each of these emphases brought a further release of the Spirit among us, and we realised that God had been preparing the ground into which this seed of anointing would be planted, so that it would produce abundant fruit.

Throughout, there was the constant expectation that we would meet with Jesus in genuine revival; that He would release His power among us in ways beyond anything we could imagine. And throughout there was concern, not only for our church but for the nation, that we would be equipped and faithful in meeting with God in such a way that we could be used by Him to bring revival to our land and beyond.

From the beginning of Kingdom Faith Church, we had

been committed to pray especially for a twenty-five-mile radius around our base in Sussex. We expected a move of God in this whole area, praying for every city, town and village; praying that every church would become open to the reviving power of God's Spirit.

We wanted Kingdom Faith Church to be a blessing to the whole area and to the nation. We wanted to bless and encourage other churches, to share with others the great riches that God was already pouring into our lives.

3

The Scenario

Nothing is more important than knowing that God has completely forgiven you. That all your sins, inadequacy and failure are forgiven and forgotten. That you have been totally accepted by Him, now and for ever.

It is one thing to believe this truth as head knowledge; it is another to know these things in your heart, so that you live in the freedom and joy that such revelation brings. Many people seek ministry when their real need is revelation of the truth about who God is and what He has accomplished for us in Jesus Christ!

Many look at themselves and do not like what they see. It does not require much self-analysis to realise that even though a person is born again and has received the gift of the Holy Spirit, he or she still sins, is prone to weakness and failure, and often feels spiritually inadequate. Even though the Christian may want to live a life pleasing to God, he feels that he constantly fails to achieve this objective. The more he looks at himself the more discouraged he becomes, especially as his failures seem to be repeated again and again. There are certain issues in his life he recognises as wrong. He makes regular decisions to amend his life in these areas and even prays that God will help him in this endeavour. And yet still the cycle of failure persists. And so he becomes resigned to the fear that he will simply have to live with his problems.

Even though the Lord blesses him in many ways, he sees such serious limitations in his prayer life and personal walk with God that his expectations of what God can and will do in him, through him and for him, are seriously limited. The reasons for this are not difficult to see. If I am conscious of my sin, failure and personal inadequacy, what is God's estimate of me? If I have a negative assessment of myself, what does He who is perfect, holy and righteous think of me? Surely His assessment must be much worse than my own? He knows all about me and I can hide nothing from Him. He knows every thought from afar, every word even before I speak it (Ps. 139:2, 4). Surely His judgement of me must be much worse than my own estimate of myself?

The Christian often reasons that, even though he is accepted by God in Christ, He cannot be very pleased with him. As a result he lacks boldness, confidence and true expectation that God will answer his prayers in supernatural, miraculous ways. He settles into a routine Christian life at a level far below that which God has designed for him. Deep down he feels himself to be spiritually inadequate – just one of God's 'also-rans'!

Talk of 'overcoming faith' seems unreal to such a Christian. He would like to have such faith, but thinks this is beyond him. Try as he may to walk in victory, failure seems to dog his footsteps. Others tell him this should not be the case; yet this only increases the sense of condemnation he feels. He reminds himself constantly that there is no condemnation for those in Christ Jesus. Even if he succeeds in projecting a smiling Christian image on the outside, nothing can hide the fact that he feels condemned to failure on the inside!

In other words, he feels trapped. Is there any way out of his dilemma? If he seeks counselling, he may find help in some ways, but probably still does not come to a place of total security in God. For most counselling concentrates on the same focus he has been obsessed with – *himself*. No matter how many times people assure him he is loved by God and accepted through Jesus, there is still the underlying question: 'Then why am I still as I am?' He can see no way out. At times he is hanging on to his faith by his fingertips. Even though there are the times when he is aware of the Lord's loving presence, the Christian life seems so hard! What is wrong?

He will not find the answer in himself, but in God; in understanding who He really is. The believer's real problem is that, for all his spiritual knowledge and experience, he has significant misunderstandings about God. And this is where revival needs to begin for him; coming to a new revelation of God Himself.

Jesus became man for a number of reasons. He came to reveal His Father's nature; to tell us by word and deed what God is really like. He came to correct our misunderstandings about God and reveal the truth to us.

Herein lies the problem. Everyone, believer or non-believer, lives with his own idea of who God is, of what this word 'God' signifies. Atheists are usually right not to believe in their ideas of God, because they have the wrong concepts of who He is. It is almost impossible to understand who God is, and not to believe in Him!

However, when a person first becomes a Christian he still has a very hazy and imperfect understanding of God's nature. He almost certainly has some fundamental misconceptions of how God views him. He projects his own negative views of himself on to God because he lacks revelation of certain vital areas of truth.

We have the Bible as God's written Word to us. This contains revelation of who He is and how He wants to relate to those who are His children. Every one of us needs to test his or her views of God against the revelation of His personality and character given us by Jesus. When we do this, we discover that many of the negative views we have of ourselves are groundless as far as God is concerned; that **He has a much higher view of us than we have of ourselves. He has accepted us more fully than we either accept ourselves, or feel accepted by others.**

Many Christians live with a false view of themselves because they have a false view of God. They do not appreciate the full nature of the wonderful things Jesus Christ has accomplished for them, taking them beyond the judgement they deserve, into His eternal life and love.

In other words, if as a believer I think that God is sitting on His throne, looking at my life and judging me for my failure to live up to His high standard, then I clearly do not understand certain things about God Himself and the wonderful nature of the gospel. For God does not treat the believer as he or she deserves, as Jesus Himself makes clear. How could God be prepared to pour such anointing on us, to come to live in us in the person of the Holy Spirit, unless He loved us and totally accepted us?

To answer this question we must sit at the feet of Jesus and listen to what He teaches us about the nature of His Father's heart, and therefore His disposition towards us. This vital revelation led us at Kingdom Faith to a new understanding of how we would experience the full blessing of revival for which we were longing.

4

The God of Mercy

Whenever Jesus taught the people He used parables to convey the truth about the Kingdom of God and the nature of the One who reigns over it. In Matthew 18 we find what is usually known as 'The Parable of the Unmerciful Servant'. There is an unmerciful servant in this parable, but he is not the central character, as Jesus Himself makes clear:

> Therefore, the kingdom of heaven is like a king who wanted to settle accounts with his servants. (v.23)

This is a parable about a king; he is the central character of the story, not the servant. Clearly in this parable the king represents God. In this story Jesus tells us something of the nature of God's heart and how He relates to the servant. It is a story about the King of Heaven.

When we look at the story with this proper emphasis, we discover a series of amazing truths about God and how He relates to us.

1. The king has the right to judge, 'to settle accounts with His servants'. This accords with much that we read in both the Old and New Testaments about God being the judge of the living and the dead.
2. The servant owed the king ten thousand talents, a vast sum of money totally beyond his competence to repay.
3. The king duly pronounced his righteous judgement: 'The

master ordered that he and his wife and his children and all that he had be sold to repay the debt.' Nobody could accuse the king of unrighteousness or injustice. The servant had acted unrighteously in getting himself into a position of such debt, and the king was justified in doing whatever he could to recover as much of the debt as possible.

4 **The servant pleads for mercy.** He falls on his knees before the king, 'Be patient with me and I will pay back everything.' This is the typical plea of anyone in debt: 'Give me more time.' This is the cry of many a businessman to his bank manager when caught in a recession or financial crisis!

5 The king, who is the servant's master, responds to this plea by taking pity on him. He had mercy on him. The Greek word means that **he was tender-hearted towards him.** So Jesus tells this story to show the nature of God's heart towards anyone who appeals to His mercy. When He takes pity, He does not merely feel sorry for those who are the object of His pity; He is moved to action. **He expresses His mercy in positive action.**

6 The king cancels the debt and releases the servant. It takes only a decision, just a word from the king, and the servant is released completely from the debt, despite its enormous size.

Whenever you sin you place yourself in debt to God. **When you appeal to His mercy, when you ask Him to forgive you, He cancels the debt. This is what it means to be forgiven by God. Every debt is cancelled! You are debt-free!**

Why? Because of the nature of the King's heart. Instead of judging you as you deserve, as He has the right to do, your appeal to Him for mercy touches His heart of compassion and He forgives you completely. **He cancels your debt and allows you to go free!**

This shows the complete nature of God's forgiveness. But it shows us also something about the nature of God

Himself. He has the right to judge, to give us what we deserve! But He chooses not to do so because He has a heart of compassion. He does not want to judge; **He wants to be merciful**!

That mercy expresses something of His loving heart. In fact, mercy is the Christian's first taste of God's love, for to be born again all his sins must be forgiven. Jesus said:

> The time has come. The kingdom of God is near. Repent and believe the good news! (Mark 1:15)

To repent is to turn to God, confessing your sins and availing yourself of His mercy. You need also to believe the good news: that God is indeed merciful and does not treat you as you deserve. He cancels your debts and lets you go free! Hallelujah! This is good news.

Receive this revelation in your heart. If you have appealed to His mercy, **He has forgiven you and has cancelled your debt**. For He teaches us in His Word:

> If we confess our sins, he is faithful and just and will forgive us our sins and purify us from all unrighteousness. (1 John 1:9)

Not only is He merciful, but He is just in showing you His mercy. In forgiving you, God is not saying that your sins do not matter; He demonstrates that His mercy is greater than your sins, that His love far outdoes any lack of love for Him!

Can such forgiveness be earned or deserved? Never! It is simply the evidence of God's merciful heart, the same heart that moved Him to send Jesus to die on the cross to make such forgiveness possible.

Is there anything God expects of those who avail themselves of this mercy? Definitely!

7 The servant on whom the king had lavished his mercy refuses to forgive the debt of a fellow-servant that is a pittance by comparison. 'Pay back what you owe me' was his attitude.

8 The fellow-servant asks for mercy in a similar fashion: 'Be patient with me, and I will pay you back' (v.29).

9 But the servant refuses to have mercy. **God is so much more merciful to us than we are prepared to be towards one another**!

10 The servant judges his fellow-servant instead of having mercy on him. He has him thrown into prison until the debt is paid.

11 The other servants are understandably outraged by this and report what has happened to the king. Remember, he is the central character in this story. So Jesus now teaches what He does in such a situation.

12 The master summons the servant: 'You wicked servant, I cancelled all that debt of yours because you begged me to. Shouldn't you have had mercy on your fellow-servant just as I had on you?'

So in showing us His great mercy, God expects us to be merciful towards others. He wants our hearts to be as His own heart. He wants to reproduce Himself in His children.

13 In anger the king cancels his forgiveness of the unmerciful servant's enormous debt. This is an aspect of the story that is often ignored!

There is no debt too great to be forgiven by God. However, having tasted of His mercy, we are expected to be merciful to others. Unwillingness to do so places us back in bondage. This is in line with what Jesus teaches elsewhere:

> For if you forgive men when they sin against you, your heavenly Father will also forgive you. But if you do not forgive men their sins, your Father will not forgive your sins. (Matt. 6:14–15)

If you refuse to forgive others, you place yourself back under judgement. That is not a clever thing to do.

Jesus shows us that God's judgement, which we clearly deserve, is tempered by His mercy. **He is prepared to be merciful to those who show mercy**.

> Blessed are the merciful, for they will be shown mercy. (Matt. 5:7)

It is clearly His intention to reproduce His mercy in those who believe in Him. 'Be merciful, just as your Father is merciful,' (Luke 6:36) says Jesus.

14 In anger, the master turns the unmerciful servant over 'to the jailers to be tortured, until he should pay back all he owed'. We do not need to spend time in pondering what the nature of the torture would be. Clearly anyone with any sense wants to avoid torture. It is enough to see that the king delivered the servant from an impossible situation. That servant's unwillingness to be merciful brought judgement upon himself; and so he returns to an impossible position. He is in prison unable to repay his debt.

15 Jesus warns: 'This is how my heavenly Father will treat each of you unless you forgive your brother from your heart' (v.35). This needs no interpretation; the meaning is clear!

This parable helps us to see that there are different sides to God's character. **Although He is merciful, He is always righteous.** He is still the judge of all men. To avail yourself of His mercy means that He does not judge you as you deserve. He freely forgives you and cancels your debt. To refuse to forgive others places you back under judgement. Jesus said:

> Do not judge, or you too will be judged. For in the

same way as you judge others, you will be judged, and with the measure you use, it will be measured to you. (Matt. 7:1–2)

God wants His forgiveness to be permanent so that the debt does not need to be restored. Having received His forgiveness, you are ready to forgive others readily.

Forgiveness is not an emotion; it is a decision. When the servant appealed to the king for mercy, he touched the king's heart. His action in cancelling the debt was a heart decision. Your forgiveness of others needs to be similar. If you wait for the right feelings you will often refuse to forgive. At the end of this parable Jesus says you must forgive from your heart; you see the need to be merciful no matter how you feel about the situation.

Forgiving others is seldom easy; but it is much easier when you know how merciful God is towards you. Then you come to the conclusion: **'If the Lord is prepared to forgive me so readily when I confess my sins to Him and appeal to His mercy, then how dare I withold forgiveness from anyone else!'**

One further thing needs to be made clear. When the king forgave the servant, it was not his intention that this should be a temporary cancelling of the debt. As far as he was concerned the matter was dealt with once and for all. It was only the unjust behaviour of the servant subsequently that necessitated the restoration of the debt by the master. His tender heart was now angry because of the servant's lack of compassion.

So when you ask God for His forgiveness, do not think that He will give you only temporary relief from your guilt. No, the scriptures teach us that He puts our sin behind His back; that He separates us from our sin as far as East is from West. **He has no desire to restore your debt; He wants you to walk in complete freedom – willing to forgive others as well as rejoicing in your freedom.**

When the Lord spoke to us afresh at Kingdom Faith

about His mercy, He began a process that went on for several weeks. We could never deserve a move of God's Spirit that would bring the full blessings and fruit of revival. This would have to be a work of His mercy!

We could not *earn* revival, no matter how much we prayed and prepared our hearts. We came to realise that He is so merciful, He would honour His promises and *give* us the revival we needed in this country.

When we prayed for the nation, we needed to believe that He would have mercy and send a move of the Holy Spirit that would change the spiritual state of the land! We would need revival for a generation, for it would take that long to bring about a spiritual change in the entire nation. God was merciful enough to do just that!

5

Completely Restored

Another parable is commonly referred to as that of the Prodigal Son, or 'The Parable of the Two Sons' (Luke 15:11–32). Both are inappropriate titles because neither of the sons is the central character in the story. Jesus began the parable by saying: 'There was a man who had two sons . . .' The father is the central character. Just as the king clearly represented God in the parable previously considered, so the father in this parable obviously represents God. Jesus is teaching us about His Father:

1. The younger son asks his father for his share of the inheritance that is due to him. **Every son in God's Kingdom has an inheritance**, which is why Paul said: 'Now if we are children, then we are heirs – heirs of God and co-heirs with Christ' (Rom. 8:17).
2. The father divided the inheritance between his two sons. **Because the younger boy asked, he received** – even though the father must have been well aware of his unreliable nature.
3. The true nature of this son is soon revealed. Having received his inheritance, he does with it what he wants. He is thoroughly selfish and totally lacking in his regard for his father's love for him.
4. He wastes all his money on riotous living and ends up doing the unthinkable for any self-respecting Jew: he has to feed pigs, animals considered unclean.

The father did not pursue the son to the city or try

to persuade him to return. He knew he had to wait patiently for his decision to come home. He did not even go searching for him while the son was feeding pigs. **He waited until such time as the son was repentant and ready to avail himself again of his father's love**.

Jesus is talking about *sons* – not outsiders of God's family, but those who belong to Him and have an inheritance. This is a parable for Christians to take to heart.

5 The younger son 'came to his senses' (v. 17). He realised that even the servants in his father's house, who have no right of inheritance, fared far better than he himself. He decides to return home – the crucial decision!

6 He does what we all do when in difficult situations. He works out what he will say!

> Father, I have sinned against heaven and against you. I am no longer worthy to be called your son; make me like one of your hired men. (v. 18–19)

7 Now the action centres on the central figure in the parable. 'While he was still a long way off, his father saw him and was filled with compassion for him' (v. 20). The father has waited patiently for the return of his son. **His attitude is not one of judgement or punishment, but of mercy and compassion**.

Whether we think of God as King or Father (and He is both), **He has only one heart – a heart of compassion**! As in the previous parable that compassion moves Him to action.

8 'He ran to his son, threw his arms around him and kissed him' (v. 20). As soon as the son takes the necessary steps to return home, the father cannot contain himself! He goes running to meet his son. He embraces him in love and kisses him as a sign of his acceptance.

9 So far the son has not said anything! He begins his prepared speech, but is unable to finish before the father

intervenes. As soon as the boy suggests he is no longer worthy to be called a son, the father cuts straight across what he is saying.

When God restores us to fellowship with Him, through the mercy of His forgiveness, we are made worthy in His sight. We are restored completely. The debt is forgiven completely.

The Christian life is about relationship with God through Jesus Christ. We are united with the One who is worthy, only by being made worthy in His sight. The sacrifice of Jesus has made that possible. Only God is worthy in and of Himself; but we are made worthy through the forgiveness of our sins.

10 The father says, 'Quick!' I love this touch in the parable. The father is moved to immediate action because of his compassion.

11 He commands the servants to do a series of things, each of which is significant. First, he commands that they bring the best robe and put it on the son. And what is the best robe? Jesus – our righteousness!

When we are forgiven we are cleansed of all unrighteousness and are clothed with Christ. He alone can make us worthy and acceptable in God's sight.

12 A ring is to be put on the son's finger. He is back in the family where he belongs!

13 The father orders sandals for his feet. **He does not want any of his sons to be in want**. Even though he had claimed his share of the inheritance previously, the son could not exhaust his father's grace and desire to give to him.

Unlike many earthly fathers, this one did not lecture his son. There was no: 'I warned you', or 'You brought all this trouble upon yourself', or, 'Before I take you back home there are some things I need to make clear to you'. **No, the father simply restored him! Freely and without condition**.

14 The father orders a celebration feast to honour the return of his son, for there is more joy in heaven over one

sinner who repents than over ninety-nine who need no repentance. The reason for the celebration is clear: 'For this son of mine was dead and is alive again; he was lost and is found' (v. 24).

15 The older son returns from his work in the fields to hear the sound of music and dancing. He is told the reason for the celebration is the return home of his brother. He is furious and refuses to join the festivities. Unlike his father, he has no heart of compassion towards his brother.

16 The father loves the older son also – so he leaves the celebration to speak with him.

17 The older son is full of his own self-righteousness. 'Look! All these years I've been slaving for you and never disobeyed your orders. Yet you never gave me even a young goat so I could celebrate with my friends' (v. 29).

This son is typical of religious people who try to please God by their performance and never lay hold of the inheritance that is theirs. The boy had never trusted his father's love and asked for a feast. If the father was willing to give the whole inheritance owed to the younger son, he would certainly have given a goat to his elder son if only he had asked!

Again we are faced with the fact that **God is far more merciful, compassionate, forgiving, loving and kind than we are to one another**.

Suppose a member of your church went off and lived with a prostitute for four years. Then one Sunday he appears at the service again. He weeps tears of genuine repentance and is clearly 'returning home'. Would your pastor say to the congregation: 'Please cancel all your plans for the rest of the day. We are going to celebrate together because our brother here has returned to the Lord?' And if the pastor did order such a feast, would you go?

All too often we are quick to judge, suspicious that the

repentance might not be real, that he might return to his sins. How wonderful that God never reacts towards us in such ways. Where would we be if God's attitude was similar when we asked for forgiveness? Instead of mercy we would find judgement. Instead of acceptance we would receive suspicion. Instead of being restored in love we would be made to fear that if we ever sinned again there would be no hope of acceptance!

Praise God that His mercy is so different from such attitudes!

18 The father reminds the older son, 'everything I have is yours' (v. 31).

We never lose anything when we forgive or extend mercy to others. We do not deprive ourselves of anything. Rather, we are enriched, and we gain a brother as well as pleasing our Father. Paul rightly exhorts us:

> Brothers, if someone is caught in a sin, you who are spiritual should restore him gently.
> But watch yourself, or you also may be tempted. (Gal. 6:1)

Jesus described Himself as being 'gentle and humble in heart' (Matt. 11:29). He wants to see that merciful, gentle, humble heart reproduced in all who honour His Name!

19 The father points out to the older son: 'We had to celebrate and be glad, because *this brother of yours* was dead and is alive again; he was lost and is found' (v. 32).

The phrase 'this brother of yours' is in direct contrast to that used by the older son when describing his brother. When speaking to the father he referred to the younger brother as '*this son of yours*'. He subtly refused to accept him as a brother. Such is the sin of self-righteous judgement!

Some Christians are prone to look down their noses in judgement and criticism at the sins of other believers.

Their attitude is: 'How terrible! I would never do such a thing.'

When the woman caught in the act of adultery was brought before Jesus, He did not say: 'Let he who has not committed adultery cast the first stone.' No, He said: 'Let he who is without *sin* cast the first stone.'

Sometimes we consider we have the right to judge someone else if we are not guilty of the same kind of sin. 'I would never do such a thing!' But this is not how Jesus looked at things. *Any* sin renders us incapable of standing in judgement on others. He made clear that the Father gave all judgement to Jesus as His Son – because He was without sin. If *all* judgement has been given to the Son by the Father, that leaves none for you!

These two parables both portray God as He really is:

> **The Lord is gracious and compassionate, slow to anger and rich in love. The Lord is good to all; he has compassion on all he has made**. (Ps. 145:8–9)

That is the nature of God's heart. He is holy and righteous at all times. He has the right to judge and condemn, but desires to show His mercy and compassion to all who call on Him.

His mercies are new every morning, for not a day goes by without our need of His mercy. We can be thankful that He so willingly extends such mercy to us. And we can willingly extend mercy and forgiveness to others instead of judging them!

There is nothing worse than sensing others are judging you, especially if they are people you love dearly. And you can sense that judgement readily enough! How wonderful to be part of a community of believers who love and accept you; who instead of judging you, pray for you!

This is not to say that God treats sin lightly. It is to realise that His mercy is so much greater than our sin. **The blood of Jesus cleanses us from every sin and enables us to be at peace with God, with others and even with ourselves.**

It is this last part that many find the most difficult. If God has forgiven you, then you have no right to refuse to forgive yourself. To do so suggests you know better than God. It indicates that you find it difficult to believe that God could forgive you so readily. It seems too good to be true that you could be restored so readily to fellowship with your heavenly Father. You feel that you deserve to be punished in some way, so you punish yourself.

Many live in false self-condemnation because they fail to believe that God has so completely forgiven and restored them.

Jesus suffered on our behalf the punishment we deserve.

> But he was pierced for our transgressions, he was crushed for our iniquities; the punishment that brought us peace was upon him, and by his wounds we are healed. (Isa. 53:5)

We feel we deserve punishment when we know we have sinned in some serious way, or feel we have failed the Lord persistently. Both the parables we have considered make it clear that God does not want to punish or judge. He honours the cry for mercy. The cleansing power of the blood of Jesus is available to all who call upon Him.

And yet there is still another subtle area of unbelief for some. They believe that God has forgiven them, for they know this to be the promise of His Word. And yet they do not truly believe they have been restored fully in their relationship with God. They think He must think ill of them because they sinned. They do not pray with conviction that He will answer their prayers because they have not walked in righteousness in some areas of their lives.

Clearly this is wrong thinking. **To suggest that God will not answer us because we sinned would be a subtle form of punishment! It would also suggest that the believer is not fully restored by His mercy, that God still does not consider him or her clean, holy and righteous in His sight.**

The prodigal was restored completely and without any punishment although he had wasted his inheritance and had sinned grievously over a prolonged period of time. Sometimes we belittle the nature of God's forgiveness! Jesus said:

> For God did not send his Son into the world to condemn the world, but to save the world through him. **Whoever believes in him is not condemned**, but whoever does not believe stands condemned already because he has not believed in the name of God's one and only Son. (John 3:17–18)

So self-condemnation is the product of unbelief.

God wants you to believe in the full nature of His mercy. **When you are forgiven, you stand in His presence, clothed with Jesus**. And He does not deal with you or withhold anything from you because you sinned. It is as if that sin had never taken place. God does not hold any grudges against you. On the Day of Judgement He will not remember those sins He has forgiven. They are erased from heaven's record books!

It is not simply that sins are forgiven. *You* are forgiven, the one who committed the sin. *You* are restored. *You* are made worthy. *You* are accepted totally in the Beloved. This is the nature of God's mercy and love towards *you*.

This revelation of God's mercy had a profound effect on us in Kingdom Faith. It is at the very heart of the gospel. As He was leading us forwards in His revival purposes, the Lord made it clear that He wanted to take us back to some of these basic truths, so that they could have a more profound effect on our lives.

This certainly happened. Subsequently, for many months I taught about God's mercy in several different nations, often to groups of pastors and leaders. Always God moved deeply in people's hearts bringing them to a fresh understanding of the extent of His mercy and the complete nature of His forgiveness. Many later testified to significant changes in their preaching and ministries as a result.

We found also that this fresh revelation of God's mercy had a positive effect on our relationships with others. All of us knew that it was wrong to harbour critical and judgemental attitudes. As a preacher, I knew how important it is to try and eradicate any such tendencies in the body of believers.

However, sometimes when you preach, those who most need to take heed seem to allow the word to pass over their heads. I have known deeply critical people say: 'That was a good word; people need to hear that!' They mean, of course, that everybody else needs to hear such a message! Their critical attitudes ensure they apply correction to others rather than themselves.

When the Lord showed us His mercy and that He expected us to extend similar mercy to others, some suddenly realised that they dare not remain critical or judgemental in their attitudes. **The truth of God's mercy towards us caused us to be more merciful to others.**

This is an important aspect of revival. Those who live in revival are ready to pray and work to see lost souls drawn into God's Kingdom. However, we will not be effective witnesses to people we judge! We need to reach out to sinners with God's mercy.

Prostitutes, swindlers and crooks did not feel threatened by Jesus. He went to eat with them, not to condemn them, but because in His love He wanted to reach out to them in His mercy. Somehow such sinners sensed that Jesus did not condemn them, but cared about them – in direct contrast to the self-righteous religious leaders of the time.

Jesus has shown you mercy that you may reach out to others in mercy and draw them into His love and acceptance. What a wonderful privilege for, no matter what their sin, God wants them to know complete forgiveness and full salvation. He wants to give them an entirely new life and make them co-heirs with Christ! What love! What mercy!

6

Mercy in Jesus's Ministry

When God speaks to you about a particular subject, it is invariably helpful to do a biblical word-study of that subject. God is by nature merciful. Various words are used in the Hebrew of the Old Testament and the Greek of the New Testament to reveal the nature of this mercy.

The Hebrew word *chesed* is used some 250 times in the Bible. It means kindness, mercy, loving-kindness, unfailing love, tenderness, faithfulness. This is a good description of the Lord's heart towards His children. **He is kind, loving, tender and faithful towards you**.

There is a refrain that runs through Psalm 136: 'His mercy endures for ever.' *Chesed* is used also in Micah 6:8:

> And what does the Lord require of you? To act justly and to love mercy and to walk humbly with your God.

His mercy endures for ever; He is always merciful and always will be. He wants you to love mercy because He loves mercy.

The Hebrew verb *rarkam* means to feel or show compassion, to love deeply, to show pity or mercy; to respond to someone tenderly, to love tenderly. It speaks of the tender love and compassion loving parents have for their child.

The Lord shows His mercy to us as the loving Father that He is; almighty, yet tender in His love for us. In the New Testament, this note of tenderness and compassion continues, as we would expect; for God's nature never changes. He is who He is.

The Greek noun *eleos* means compassion, tender mercy, kindness, beneficence, and is an outward manifestation of pity. It is used of God:

> His mercy extends to those who fear him, from generation to generation. (Luke 1:50)

It is also used of men when Jesus quotes the scripture: 'I desire mercy, not sacrifice' (Matt. 12:7, quoting Hos. 6:6).

The verb *eleeo* means to show kindness and concern for someone in serious need; to feel compassion for another and to have pity on him or her.

God's mercy moves Him to action. So we would expect to see Jesus acting in mercy, expressing this compassion by practical action in the meeting of people's needs. Because Jesus had compassion, He wanted to do whatever was necessary to meet the needs of those around Him.

The adverb *eleaman* is the word used when He says: 'Blessed are the merciful, for they will be shown mercy.' As with Jesus, someone who has mercy will want to express this quality in positive action. So to be merciful is much more than an attitude of heart or mind, or a particular disposition towards someone else. **True compassion, mercy or pity moves people to action**.

God does not only feel merciful towards you because He is merciful; He wants to express that mercy again and again in positive action, and He does this in a number of different ways. We see the evidence of this in Jesus's ministry.

In the Gospels there are four principal ways in which Jesus expressed God's mercy to His people.

1 IN FORGIVENESS

We have seen that Jesus taught that God has a merciful heart, whether we view Him as King or Father. His willingness to forgive angered His opponents who were hard-hearted and judgemental.

Through His death on the cross, the forgiveness He showed to those who came to Him is made available to everyone of every generation who turns to Him for mercy. He expressed His love and compassion for us in making the ultimate sacrifice for us. The Sinless One died for sinners that they might be freed from their sins and saved from the punishment they deserve.

We shall take a more detailed look at the cross in the next chapter. But first let us see other ways in which Jesus expressed mercy and compassion during His earthly ministry, before He came to the cross.

2 JESUS TAUGHT THE PEOPLE

Everything Jesus did, He did from the heart. We cannot imagine Him doing anything superficially.

> When Jesus landed and saw a large crowd, **he had compassion on them**, because they were like sheep without a shepherd. So he began teaching them many things. (Mark 6:34)

His heart went out to the people when He saw they were not being pastored properly. And so He set about doing the task Himself by teaching them.

It is impossible for people to be pastored correctly without anointed teaching of the truth of God's Word, and the example of faith in the scriptures. Those who do not teach the Bible as truth do not have God's compassion towards others. They may have human compassion, but not God's mercy. For God expresses His mercy in Jesus, who is the Truth, the Word and our life. **Only faith in Him can set people free and enable them to be fed properly. He is the Bread of Life; He is the Bread sent from heaven that we might feed on His words and live.**

Some Christians try to survive in congregations where God's Word is not taught or lived, instead of going where they can be fed properly and built up in the life and truth of Jesus Christ. Only then can they be fruitful in the way God intends for His glory. He does not expect people to express what they have not first received.

Jesus saw the need for the people to be taught the truth, the good news. He wanted to feed them spiritually. But He also wanted to feed them physically.

One of the key elements of the move of God we have been enjoying in Kingdom Faith is the teaching and confessing of the Word of truth. You can read more of this in my book: *The Truth that Sets You Free*. Jesus insisted that only the truth will set us free – not ministry techniques based on looking at ourselves and our past. The Word of truth points us to the facts of what Jesus has done for us and our place in Him.

Christians need to hear and believe His words, store them up in their hearts, speak them over their own lives, encourage other Christians with these words of truth and declare them boldly to the world.

The Holy Spirit is the Spirit of Truth. He guides us into the truth. He takes the things of Jesus and declares them to us. **Any true ministry in the Holy Spirit will, therefore, direct us to the truth of God's Word. The Spirit and Word work together that we may live in the glorious freedom of the sons of God. Anointing from God is essential to communicate God's Word to others in ways that will bring them life and liberty.**

3 JESUS PROVIDED FOR THE PEOPLE

After listening to His teaching, Jesus did not want to send the people away hungry. He said:

> **I have compassion for these people;** they have already been with me three days and have nothing to eat. (Matt. 15:32)

And so the miracle of the feeding of the multitude took place. Jesus took the insignificant offering of a boy's picnic and fed thousands. This action was the result of His heart of compassion and demonstrates that God's desire to provide for us is expressed in practical ways, even if miracles are necessary to accomplish this.

God's heart does not change; He is always compassionate. So He always wants to provide for His beloved ones. We pray, therefore, to the Lord of mercy, the One who has compassion on us, who desires to meet our needs according to his glorious riches in Christ Jesus (Phil. 4:19).

When Jesus taught the disciples the prayer of faith (Mark 11:22–24), the first thing He told them to do was to 'Have faith in God'. This seems so self-evident that we might wonder why He said it.

Jesus was aware that it is possible to have more faith in the problem or the need than in Him! But He was doing more than telling the disciples to trust God rather than their circumstances. He was telling them to trust in who God is, the Lord of mercy, who is full of compassion. **They are praying to the One who wants to fulfil their needs by positive action, even though they are unworthy and deserve nothing.**

Therefore, when we pray we can be full of confidence. 'Ask and it will be given to you . . . for everyone who asks receives' (Matt. 7:7–8). Obviously this means asking in faith, trusting in the One to whom you pray. Therefore, Jesus said: 'Whatever you ask for in prayer, believe that you have received it, and it will be yours' (Mark 11:24).

It is not a question of coming up with the right prayer formula, but of trusting in the mercy of God. Again and again we see this evidenced in those who came to Jesus for help.

4 JESUS HEALED THE PEOPLE

On several occasions when people approached Jesus with a healing need, they called upon God's mercy. For example blind Bartimaeus cried out: **'Jesus, Son of David, have mercy**

on me!' When others rebuked him, he shouted all the more, **'Son of David, have mercy on me!'** (Mark 10:47–48).

Jesus asked him what he wanted, to which he replied that he wanted his sight back. Jesus said to him: 'Go, your faith has healed you.' Immediately he received his sight and followed Jesus along the road (v. 52).

This is in line with several other incidents where Jesus made it clear that the power of faith in Him brings healing. But what faith is Bartimaeus expressing? He doesn't come with the usual expression: 'Oh Lord, I believe, I really believe.' He doesn't come with a faith formula, but with a cry in his heart, 'Have mercy on me.'

This is a cry of faith because he expects Jesus to express God's mercy to him by healing him. He recognises that **he could never deserve or earn such a wonderful answer to prayer; it would have to be the work of God's mercy.**

However, this is not an isolated incident. The first healing miracle recorded is that of the leper who came with a very tentative faith.

> A man with leprosy came to him and begged him on his knees, 'If you are willing, you can make me clean.' (Mark 1:40)

What was Jesus's response to such an appeal?

> **Filled with compassion,** Jesus reached out his hand and touched the man. 'I am willing,' he said. 'Be clean.' Immediately the leprosy left him and he was cured. (Mark 1:41–42)

So even when our faith seems tentative, God is willing to show us mercy. A Canaanite woman, like Bartimaeus, appealed to Jesus:

> 'Lord, Son of David, **have mercy on me!** My daughter is suffering terribly from demon possession.' (Matt. 15:22)

She did not belong 'to the lost sheep of Israel'. Yet she believed that only crumbs from the table would be sufficient to heal her daughter. Jesus's heart went out to her:

> 'Woman, you have great faith! Your request is granted.' And her daughter was healed from that very hour. (Matt. 15:28)

When Jesus came down from the Mount of Transfiguration He found nine of His disciples unable to heal an epileptic boy. The boy's father appealed to Jesus:

> A man approached Jesus and knelt before him. **'Lord, have mercy on my son,'** he said. Jesus rebuked the demon, and it came out of the boy, and he was healed from that moment. (Matt. 17:14–15, 18)

Notice how, when people came to Jesus asking for mercy, they came humbly, kneeling before Him in reverent submission.

These incidents show that because He is merciful God wants to heal the sick:

> When Jesus landed and saw a large crowd, **he had compassion on them and healed their sick.** (Matt. 14:14)

So in compassion, Jesus not only forgives sin, He pastors the people by teaching them, He provides for their needs by feeding them and He sets them free by healing them!

Jesus was often in confrontation with the Pharisees and leading religionists of His time. One of the issues that was central to this confrontation was their lack of mercy. When they criticised Him for eating with the swindling tax-collectors and sinners, He said:

> Go and learn what this means: 'I desire mercy, not sacrifice.' For I have not come to call the righteous, but sinners. (Matt. 9:13)

The Pharisees' external religious observances could never please God, who looks upon the heart. They considered themselves ritually clean and acceptable to God because they were fastidious in obeying their religious traditions; but Jesus perceived otherwise. When they criticised His disciples for picking grain on the Sabbath, Jesus told them:

> If you had known what these words mean, 'I desire mercy, not sacrifice', you would not have condemned the innocent. (Matt. 12:7)

He was angry with the Pharisees when they criticised Him for healing on the Sabbath:

> He looked round at them in anger and, deeply distressed at their stubborn hearts, said to the man, 'Stretch out your hand.' He stretched it out, and his hand was completely restored. Then the Pharisees went out and began to plot with the Herodians how they might kill Jesus. (Mark 3:5–6)

Such is the fruit of a love of religious traditions, placed above love for God and for people. Again we see how a lack of mercy angered Jesus.

> Woe to you, teachers of the law and Pharisees, you hypocrites! You give a tenth . . . But you have neglected the more important matters of the law – justice, mercy and faithfulness. You should have practised the latter, without neglecting the former. You blind guides! (Matt. 23:23–24)

It is clear that no amount of religious observance can make up for an unclean heart!

Jesus told the parable of the Good Samaritan to show that God expects those who honour His Name to reach out to others with mercy in practical ways. Neither the priest nor the Levite were prepared to go to the aid of the injured man, only a Samaritan, one considered an outcast.

When Jesus asked which of the three was the true neighbour, the expert in the law replied, **'The one who had mercy on him'. To which Jesus replied, 'Go, and do likewise.'**

The religious leaders regularly criticised Jesus for healing on the Sabbath, eating with prostitutes and tax-collectors and generally caring for the outcasts. They stood in judgement on such people. They were so full of self-righteousness, they simply condemned them as sinners and had no time for them.

Jesus came to earth as the truly Righteous One, holy and good. You would think that the prostitutes, crooks and sinners would want to avoid Him. And yet these were the very people that were drawn to Him. Why? Because He had a heart of mercy towards them.

Unlike the Pharisees, He did not condemn them out of hand but reached out to them. He gave them hope; He offered them new life and showed them that they did not need to remain the victims of their own sin or the situations in which they lived. Here was the One who could judge them, but who chose not to do so. **His heart was full of compassion for them and He wanted to reach them with the truth that would set them free.**

On the other hand, the Pharisees rejected the truth in favour of their own religious traditions. Ultimately they even crucified the Truth!

How the heart of God, which Jesus displays, differs from the heart of man. We must learn from this, not only that He wants us to have a heart after His own heart, but also to think of Him as He really is. **In coming to Him we come humbly to the One who is always ready to be merciful and compassionate, who wants to provide for us, support us, meet our needs and even heal us.**

We do not come to one who wants to judge us, criticise and put us down. He reserves His anger and judgement for those who reject mercy in favour of their religious observances and traditions; those who are full of their own self-sufficiency and self-righteousness.

When we approach God in prayer, we come to 'the throne of grace with confidence, so that we may receive mercy and find grace to help us in our time of need' (Heb. 4:16). Because Jesus died for you on the cross, you have access to the throne of God. His mercy and grace await you every time you pray!

7

The Mercy of the Cross

Preaching about the cross is prevalent in times of revival, for the Holy Spirit points us to the truth that it was at Calvary that Jesus met our every need.

The Lord said to Moses: 'I will have mercy on whom I have mercy, and I will have compassion on whom I have compassion' (Exod. 33:19, quoted by Paul in Rom. 9:15). Does this mean that God is selective in only wanting to be merciful to some? No. **He has provided mercy for all mankind in what He did for us on the cross**.

This does not mean that all will avail themselves of this mercy. He wills all men to be saved, even though He knows that many will reject His offer of mercy and so will not be saved. God has provided the means of salvation in Jesus for all who turn to Him with repentance and faith; but He does not force anyone to accept Jesus. He awaits the willing response of the heart. If people like the Pharisees reject Him and the mercy He offers, they condemn themselves by their unbelief.

The mercy that was available to those among whom Jesus lived in the days of His humanity is now made available to men and women of every generation through the cross.

In His love and desire to be merciful, God could not overlook the serious nature of sin. He is righteous as well as merciful. Sin alienates and separates men from God. It disrupts the fellowship with Him that was His intention for mankind. Jesus came to restore that fellowship, to end the separation between God and man, and make us one with Him.

In righteousness God had to judge sin and the sinners responsible for it. He could not declare a general amnesty, giving the impression that sin doesn't matter or doesn't have serious spiritual consequences. His just and righteous judgement on sin is death. This is what the sinner deserves. And that death has eternal consequences: eternal separation from God.

This is not what God wants, but it is His wholly justified judgement on sinners. He never wants people to sin, even though He allows them to do so. He wants a relationship of love with every man, woman and child. It is impossible to force anyone to love. So God had to create us with free will, the ability to choose what we will do: love or hate, obey or disobey, be merciful or self-righteous.

Sin is the abuse of our free will. It is making wrong choices, wrong decisions which lead to wrong actions and wrong relationships. It is choosing to please self rather than God.

Instead of judging sinners in the way they deserve, God sent His Son to die for them, to set them free by His mercy. For ultimately mercy is God choosing to deal with us, not as we deserve, but as Jesus deserves. He has become our substitute on the cross. We could not have someone acting for us who had not shared our humanity and been subject to all the temptations we experience.

The difference between Jesus and us is that He did not sin. He always made the right choices, choosing to please His Father rather than Himself. He made it clear that He had not come to do His own will, but the will of Him who sent Him. He lived in perfect submission to the Father. He spoke no words of His own, only the words His Father gave Him to speak; He did nothing of Himself, but only the things He saw His Father doing.

Although He was tempted in every way, as we are, He did not sin. And so He could offer His life as a sacrifice to the Father on our behalf – the sinless One giving His life for sinners, the Righteous for the unrighteous, the Holy for the unholy, the Perfect for the imperfect.

Jesus had to share our weakness. Our sacrifice had to be as weak as we are in our humanity, and yet still remain obedient to God in all things.

But why was a sacrifice necessary? Because God's righteous judgement on sin had to be satisfied so that He could display the mercy that was in His heart.

God will never deny Himself. He is always prepared to be merciful, but He is also righteous in all He does. He could not deny His righteousness in order to be merciful. He had to satisfy His righteousness, His justice, His love and His mercy, all at the same time.

His just judgement on sin is death. So someone had to suffer the death we deserve, the punishment for our sins. The death of a sinner could not be efficacious for other sinners. The sacrifice had to be of someone tempted, but sinless. He would die for us and bear the punishment we deserve.

So the sacrifice of Jesus satisfies completely God's righteous demands; it satisfies His justice. **He has shown that sin does matter, and in love for us has taken the penalty of our sin upon Himself**.

What Jesus did on the cross was for all mankind, therefore. The scripture is clear that Christ died for all (2 Cor. 5:15). If one man has died, then all mankind has died (2 Cor. 5:14).

So in His mercy God deliberately sent His Son to die on behalf of all sinners, of all mankind.

Every man, woman and child of every generation was involved in that work of the cross. God's mercy, His forgiveness and eternal acceptance, are thereby made available to all. But only those who put their faith in what Jesus did on that cross avail themselves of His mercy. **All died in Christ, but only those who believe in Him are raised to new life with Him**.

And yet the matter is not quite so simple, for Jesus said: 'No one can come to me unless the Father who sent me draws him, and I will raise him up at the last day' (John

6:44). 'No one can come to me unless the Father has enabled him' (John 6:65).

God has made Jesus the only means of salvation. No one can come to the Father except through the cross and resurrection of Jesus Christ. Those who believe in the cross of Jesus experience the mercy of God's forgiveness. They are cleansed of all their sins and are given a new life in Him.

And yet we need the mercy of God even to avail ourselves of His mercy. We cannot come to repentance and faith without the Father calling us, choosing us for Himself, revealing the nature of our sin to us by the convicting power of the Holy Spirit and then making us a new creation when we are born again.

Without that new birth we cannot belong to God's Kingdom. He alone can give us this new birth! We could never deserve it or earn such a gift. It is His merciful and gracious work alone.

As a believer, you can be thankful that God has been merciful to you. He has opened your eyes to the truth and given you new life, abundant life, life in all its fullness.

And yet this new life did not come to you until first God had justly judged your sin. The wonderful truth is that Jesus took the penalty of that judgement upon Himself. **He literally died for you to save you from the punishment you deserved. He set you free from sin, from the burden of guilt, from Satan's domain, from the just punishment for sin and instead He gave you His own life. What a wonderful work of His mercy! He did not treat you as you deserved**.

Perhaps at first you resisted the truth of the gospel, you refused to submit to His Lordship, to acknowledge your sins and your need of His forgiveness. Perhaps you wanted to hold on to your life for yourself, instead of yielding yourself to Him to live for His purposes and glory. Yet in His love He persisted with you.

It was not enough for Christ to die for you. The Father then had to draw you to the cross so that you could become His own child. So the entire work of salvation is God's alone.

You could not have salvation without Jesus dying for you. You could not have salvation without the Father drawing you to Himself through the cross. You could not have salvation without the Holy Spirit convicting you of sin and then, once forgiven, coming to live in you. So the whole work of salvation is God's and His alone. You can only be thankful for His mercy and grace.

This work of the cross had to deal decisively with Satan's work as well as our sinfulness. Paul says of Jesus:

> Having disarmed the powers and authorities, he made a public spectacle of them, triumphing over them by the cross. (Col. 2:15)

Because every righteous demand of God is met in Jesus, Satan has no just claim upon any who belong to Christ. **Jesus is our righteousness, our holiness and redemption. We are His and His alone. We belong to God and none shall snatch us from His hand**.

The devil cannot accuse God of injustice by saying that our sins have gone unpunished, for Jesus has taken that punishment on our behalf.

Because the work of the cross was accomplished for all men, any who come to Jesus with repentance and faith must be saved by Him. The devil knows this and therefore tries to hold people in his domain by encouraging them to reject Jesus. Paul says he has blinded the minds of unbelievers so that they do not perceive the truth. They do not appreciate the dire, eternal consequences of their sins. Or they imagine falsely that all will go to heaven regardless of what they believe, or the way they live. Or they think they can earn their own way to God through their religious practices or good deeds. All this is deception, one of the devil's weapons.

Jesus, by comparison, is the Truth and only He is the Way to the Father.

> For he has rescued us from the dominion of darkness and brought us into the kingdom of the Son he loves, in whom we have redemption, the forgiveness of sins. (Col. 1:13–14)

We needed someone to redeem us. Jesus has literally purchased men for God by His own blood. He has paid the price for us so that we might no longer belong to Satan or even to ourselves, but to Him. 'You are not your own,' says Paul, 'You were bought at a price' (1 Cor. 6:20). And that price was the blood Jesus shed for you. Therefore you are now to 'honour God with your body'. You do not live for yourself (for that is the hallmark of Satan's domain); you live for Jesus, for this is the evidence of belonging to His Kingdom. And in living for Him, you live for others. You show them mercy, just as God has shown you mercy. You love others because He loves you. You give to others because He is so generous to you.

And you want to make His mercy known to others who are still in bondage. For the Father uses those who belong to His Kingdom to draw others to Jesus, to the work of the cross and to salvation. It is for this reason that Jesus said: 'As the Father has sent me, so do I send you.'

We reveal God's mercy not only by talking about it, but by demonstrating it, as Jesus did, through our willingness not to judge but to love, forgive and accept others. **In mercy we forgive. In mercy we share the truth with others. In mercy we reach out to those in need. In mercy we obey His command to heal the sick.**

We can have no righteousness of our own. We are clothed with Jesus. *He* is our righteousness. We have put on Christ. We live in Him. When God looks upon us now as believers, He does not see us apart from Christ, separated from Him. **He sees us living in Him, made totally acceptable because we live in the One who is totally accepted. We are 'accepted in the Beloved'. We have no acceptance of our own; no righteousness of our own. We are accepted in Him and He is our righteousness.**

This means I do not have to try to please God through my own efforts or performance. He does not say that He gives me salvation on a trial basis, and I will lose that salvation if I do not perform to a certain standard; for that would still be saying that I could only be saved ultimately through my own works. No, **I can only be saved by His work, and His work alone; through His mercy and His mercy alone**!

Even though I am in Christ I am still able to sin and sometimes choose to please self instead of Him. And yet God does not judge me or throw me out of His Kingdom. He continues to show me His mercy every day. So if I confess my sin, He is faithful and just to forgive me and cleanse me of all unrighteousness. He restores me to the righteous state that is mine in Christ.

He will always honour the blood of His Son. He will always be faithful and just towards those who are part of His new covenant sealed with the blood of Jesus. He will never deny Jesus. He will never deny me because I am in Him, and my trust is in Him.

Our testimony needs to be similar to Paul's:

> I have been crucified with Christ and I no longer live, but Christ lives in me. The life I live in the body, I live by faith in the Son of God, who loved me and gave himself for me. I do not set aside the grace of God, for if righteousness could be gained through the law, Christ died for nothing. (Gal. 2:20–21)

All you or I can do is to trust and rejoice in the mercy and grace of God. Paul exhorts the Romans:

> Therefore, I urge you, brothers, in view of God's mercy, to offer your bodies as living sacrifices, holy and pleasing to God – this is your spiritual act of worship. (Rom. 12:1)

Our response to the wonderful mercy of God is to let Him do with our bodies what is pleasing to Him. It is not enough to say you give Him your heart. Many live in spiritual unreality by having such an attitude. If our hearts belong to the Lord because we appreciate the mercy He has shown us, then we will want to use our bodies to show His mercy to others: to speak and act with tenderheartedness, with compassion and kindness – in practical ways, as Jesus did.

In mercy He forgave. So in mercy we forgive.
In mercy He made His body a sacrifice for us. So in mercy our bodies become living sacrifices.
In mercy He taught the people. So in mercy (not judgement) we share the truth of His Word with others.
In mercy He provided for people. And so with similar compassion we reach out to those in need.
In mercy He healed the sick. And so in mercy we obey His commission and command to heal the sick in His Name.

And when we show mercy to others we are to do so cheerfully (Rom. 12:8), not with begrudging forgiveness or acceptance. James warns us that 'judgement without mercy will be shown to anyone who has not been merciful' (Jas. 2:13). So we do not have any option in this matter. But James continues: 'Mercy triumphs over judgement!'

God wants this to be evidenced in your life, in your attitudes towards others; that even when you are tempted to judge, mercy will instead triumph. You will be a much happier person if this is the case.

We are to clothe ourselves with compassion (Col. 3:12). Paul could tell Timothy:

> I was shown mercy so that in me, the worst of sinners, Christ Jesus might display his unlimited patience as an example for those who would believe on him and receive eternal life. (1 Tim. 1:16)

It is wonderful to live daily in the knowledge that God has a heart of mercy towards you. That even when you sin or fail

Him, He is ready to forgive. That when He forgives you He keeps no record of your wrong, but treats you as one who is living in His Beloved Son.

God does not give revival to His people for their own satisfaction and enjoyment, but to enable them to be more effective in communicating the gospel to the world. Therefore an important part of that revival purpose is to touch and change believers' hearts, giving them a deeper love and compassion for others, especially the lost – those who do not have a saving knowledge of Jesus Christ.

He will anoint His children with the mustard seed of multiplication, but that seed needs to fall into hearts that are willing to please Him by obeying the great commission to make disciples of all nations. Every Christian has a part to play in that commission that Jesus gives to the whole Church.

The more you are grateful for your own salvation, the more you will be prepared to pray and work for the salvation of others! You will want them to know of the amazing truth of the cross, that Jesus has done everything necessary for their forgiveness, to see them liberated in spirit, soul and body.

8

'Lord, Have Mercy'

If we know God to be merciful, then we need to avail ourselves of that mercy. We have seen that when people came to Jesus for help, they often appealed to His mercy. This was nothing new. The Psalms are full of encouragement to pray to God as the Lord of mercy, that He will not deal with us as we deserve, but according to His loving-kindness. David says:

> The Lord has heard my cry for mercy; the Lord accepts my prayer. (Ps. 6:9)

When in grave difficulty, David appeals to God's mercy:

> O Lord, see how my enemies persecute me! Have mercy and lift me up from the gates of death. (Ps. 9:13)

Even when he seems cut off from the Lord's presence, he cries out for mercy:

> In my alarm I said, 'I am cut off from your sight!' Yet you heard my cry for mercy when I called to you for help. (Ps. 31:22)

As with those who came to Jesus, David understood that God's works of healing and restoration are the outworking of His mercy:

> I said, 'O Lord, have mercy on me; heal me, for I have sinned against you.' (Ps. 41:4)

When David had sinned grievously by committing adultery and being responsible for murder, he cried:

> Have mercy on me, O God, according to your unfailing love; according to your great compassion blot out my transgressions. (Ps. 51:1)

Mercy is the first expression of God's love that we experience. It is impossible to know in your heart that He loves you without tasting this mercy.

In any church there are those who find great difficulty in believing that God loves them. They constantly look to others to give them reassurance of His love. This gives temporary encouragement, but does not deal with the heart of their problem. They do not know His love because they do not believe truly in His mercy. **To believe in God's mercy is to believe in His total forgiveness and full acceptance – regardless of what you have been or have done**!

Without knowing His mercy a person cannot know the love of God. **Once a person knows His mercy, he or she will never question His love**. That is the power His mercy has on us, because we then appreciate that His love for us does not depend on what we are, or what we do or don't do, but on His own nature, His own heart of love and mercy.

David knows that, despite the gravity of his sin, he will teach transgressors God's ways, and sinners will turn back to him, once God has had mercy on him and restored him (Ps. 51:13). God's forgiveness completely cleanses him of sin, restores him to a place of righteousness and enables him to teach sinners. What a turn-around!

The challenge of faith is to believe that God forgives you immediately, no matter how grave the sin you confess to Him. He does not delay His forgiveness, or insist on a penance or period of restitution. He forgives.

> I love the Lord, for he heard my voice; he heard my cry for mercy. (Ps. 116:1)

In Proverbs we read:

> He who conceals his sins does not prosper, but whoever confesses and renounces them finds mercy. (Prov. 28:13)

God does not want us to be trapped in the repetition of the same sins over and over again, even though in His mercy He forgives us whenever we ask Him. He wants us to renounce the sin, to turn away from it. This requires a change of heart and mind on our part, which is the true meaning of repentance.

In His mercy God will not only forgive, but will give the grace to resist temptation and walk in His righteous ways. We do not always want to do this, for the sins that persist in our lives are those we enjoy, even if we hate ourselves for enjoying them. The Lord knows us through and through and is infinitely patient with us.

> Let the wicked forsake his way and the evil man his thoughts. Let him turn to the Lord, and he will have mercy on him, and to our God, for he will freely pardon. (Isa. 55:7)

His mercy does not end with the initial act of forgiveness we receive when we first turn to Him. He delights to show mercy (Mic. 7:18). Even when Israel was persistently disobedient to the Lord, He did not abandon His people but had compassion on them.

> Because of your great compassion you did not abandon them in the desert. By day the pillar of cloud did not cease to guide them on their path, nor the pillar of fire by night to shine on the way they were to take. (Neh. 9:19)

The Lord kept providing for His people despite the disobedience and periods of rebellion.

During 'desert experiences' God seems remote, prayer difficult and reading of His Word unrewarding; zeal and fervour for Him have gone. Yet still He loves, is merciful, gracious and continues to provide for us. He leads us through such times and brings us once again into rich pastures. He teaches us to trust Him in the difficult times, as well as in those periods when everything seems to flow easily. He 'forgives all your sins and heals all your diseases'. He 'redeems your life from the pit and crowns you with love and compassion' (Ps. 103:3–4).

This is wonderful truth. God has not only forgiven you, **He has crowned you with love and compassion.** You can wear that crown every day of your life. He has given it to you. He will never remove either His love or His mercy. They belong together and they are yours permanently. Yes, even if you get into major disasters such as those in which David found himself, you can still be confident of His mercy, for He never changes. He is '*full* of compassion' (Ps. 116:5). 'He has compassion on all he has made' (Ps. 145:9).

> **Yet the Lord longs to be gracious to you; he rises to show you compassion.** (Isa. 30:18)

In His compassion He guides His people and leads them beside springs of water (Isa. 49:10). Through His prophet, God gives us this assurance:

> Can a mother forget the baby at her breast and have no compassion on the child she has borne? Though she may forget, I will not forget you! (Isa. 49:15)

Receive this truth personally. **God will never forget you.** You are always in His thoughts. He keeps you continually in His love, and never fails to be merciful towards you.

> 'Though the mountains be shaken and the hills be removed, yet my unfailing love for you will not be shaken nor my covenant of peace be removed,' says the Lord, who has compassion on you. (Isa. 54:10)

That same compassion does not extend to God's enemies, to those who deliberately oppose Him, but to those who belong to Him.

Does God ever punish His children? He certainly disciplines those He loves, but only to bring them back into line so that He may lavish His rich blessings upon them in the way He desires. For those who choose their own ways instead of His deprive themselves.

Always remember that He is merciful by nature. He does not want to judge or condemn. He sent Jesus because He wants to forgive you, restore you, bless you and even live within you.

> He does not treat us as our sins deserve or repay us according to our iniquities. For as high as the heavens are above the earth, so great is his love for those who fear him; as far as the east is from the west, so far has he removed our transgressions from us. As a father has compassion on his children, so the Lord has compassion on those who fear him. (Ps. 103:10–13)

What love! What mercy! What compassion!

9

In Him

In His mercy God has done more than forgive and accept you. He has taken hold of your life and has placed you in His Son, Jesus Christ.

> It is because of him that you are in Christ Jesus, who has become for us wisdom from God – that is, our righteousness, holiness and redemption. (1 Cor. 1:30)

This shows the full extent of God's mercy for us. First He sends His Son to die for us, to suffer the punishment that we deserve for our sins. Not only did He take our sins to the cross, He took us, the sinners, to the cross that we might die in Him.

This is difficult to understand with your reason because you are dealing here with supernatural truth. Your reason is natural; God's truth is supernatural.

God placed you in Christ. So when He went to the cross, you went with Him. When He died, you died. You appropriate this great truth when you put your faith in Him. This is what water baptism signifies: that in Christ you are dead and lie buried with Him.

However, God's purpose is not to leave us dead and buried, but to raise us to new life in Christ. Jesus rose from the dead. And so **those who put their faith in what He did on the cross are raised to new life in Him**. He then places His Spirit within believers to enable them to live that new life.

This much is commonly stated among Christians. We now live the new risen life in Jesus Christ. This is wonderful truth. What God has accomplished for us in Christ is more wonderful still.

When we confess our sins we are forgiven by God and cleansed from all unrighteousness. This restores us to a state of righteousness, of being in right standing, or right relationship, with Him. Many seem to think that God gives the believer a righteousness of his own, and he is then expected to live according to that righteousness. It is a matter of great concern to him that he persistently fails to do so, for every believer still sins and is prone to failure. He is in a dilemma: 'If God has made me righteous, why do I still have these unrighteous desires and thoughts? Why do I still say and do those things that obviously are not right?'

This constant failure can easily lead to defeatist attitudes: 'It is all beyond me. I am just a failure.'

Paul tells us that God chose the foolish, the weak, the lowly, even the despised. Many identify readily enough with these negatives. They seem to accord with their failure syndromes!

But why should God choose such seemingly weak and ineffective people? Paul gives us the answer. They are to 'shame the wise,' 'shame the strong', to nullify the things that are' – to change the circumstances around them. Obviously foolish, weak, lowly people are not going to have such a radical effect by dependence on their own ability. And obviously God does not intend those He calls to remain foolish and ineffective.

So how does He effect this radical transformation in the believer? He places him in Christ Jesus. And what effect does this have? Jesus Himself becomes the believer's wisdom. God does not simply impart wisdom to you; **Jesus becomes your wisdom**, your wisdom from God.

What form does this wisdom take? God knows your natural weakness and failure. If He was simply to impart righteousness to you, and then tell you that your on-going relationship with Him was dependent on walking perfectly in that righteousness, you would have no hope. He knows that there will be times of sin and failure. In His mercy He forgives and restores you to *His* righteousness.

So in His wisdom, He gave Jesus to be your righteousness. You are clothed with righteousness because you are clothed with Christ. You have put on the Lord Jesus Christ, and all His virtue has become your virtue. Your acceptance before God is dependent on what He has done, not on what you do! You are in right relationship with God, not because you have succeeded in living without any sin, but because He cleanses you from all sin, all unrighteousness.

Jesus is your righteousness and He never sins. He never fails. He is never unrighteous. This means that **your righteousness does not depend on your performance, but on your position in Christ! You are righteous only because God has made His Son your righteousness. He has placed you in the Righteous One and you live in Him.**

Does this imply that it doesn't matter if you sin? No, because God tells you to abide in Christ, to live out your life in Him, in His love. He wants you to live in righteousness.

However, the more you trust in your position in Christ the more readily you will be able to do this. **And you can always be sure of God's mercy and forgiveness when you fail because of your position in the Righteous One.**

Many Christians do not think of themselves day by day as being in Christ, the Righteous One.

They may know that doctrinally this is their position; but they have never learned to live according to that position. They may think of themselves as being in Christ in the sense of being in His presence when they pray; but at other times they think of themselves as being out of His immediate presence. They know the Spirit is within them to help them. Yet because they fail, they think of themselves as separate from Christ, rather than living in Him.

Because Christ is your righteousness and you are clothed with Him, God sees you in Him, rather than in your weakness and failure. When you go out in public, you do not walk around naked; you put clothes on. Spiritually your clothes are Jesus Christ Himself. Underneath the clothes you are naked before God. But just as other people do not see you naked, so God has chosen to put you into Christ so that He sees you clothed with Him. He is your righteousness.

Even when you sin, Jesus is still your righteousness. This is the mercy of God. Your sin does not affect your position in Christ. God does not throw you out of Christ because you have sinned and failed Him. **He draws you to repentance, forgives you and cleanses you from all unrighteousness so that once again you can reflect the righteousness of Jesus.**

God did know what He was getting when He chose you to belong to Him! He can see the end from the beginning. Even if you go right away from His purposes for a time, He still restores you to righteousness as soon as you turn back to Him. His mercy is greater than your sin.

This does not mean that we are to have a careless view of sin. It was sin that made the crucifixion of Jesus necessary. But we need never be despondent. God knows that, even with the Holy Spirit living within us, we are not going to attain perfection in the way we live, even though that is to be our aim. **But He ensures that we are always acceptable in His sight because our righteous state before Him depends on Jesus, not on ourselves.**

You are accepted 'in the Beloved'. You do not have an acceptance of your own. It is completely erroneous to think that God 'accepts you as you are'. If that were the case, there would have been no need for Jesus's birth, suffering and crucifixion.

You are completely, fully, perfectly accepted 'in the Beloved', in Jesus Christ. You do not have a righteousness of your own, nor do you need one, because Jesus Christ is your righteousness. You do not have to seek some acceptability of yourself because you are already totally accepted by God because you are in Christ, who never sinned and has pleased the Father in every way. You are considered righteous before

God, because Jesus is righteous; you are accepted because He is fully acceptable.

So your relationship with God does not depend on you, but on the fact that by His mercy He has placed you in Christ so that His standing before God becomes your standing. What wonderful truth!

It was important to teach the new church at Kingdom Faith these basic biblical truths. And to keep repeating such teaching until these truths gripped people's hearts. For any church that is going to experience revival needs to be a church living by faith in God's Word. Not only would believing the truth enable people to live free from false condemnation, but they would also be able to help the steady stream of new Christians who needed to appreciate fully the work that Jesus had done for them on the cross, that they were completely forgiven, made a new creation in Christ and righteous in God's sight!

You, too, need to understand these truths and rejoice that through the mercy of God you are fully forgiven, accepted and made righteous before God!

Jesus is also your holiness. You can strive to have a holiness of your own and will always fail. The more you strive, the more legalistic you are likely to become, and less like Jesus in heart! He is your holiness, your sanctification. **God considers you holy because you are in Him.**

He did not put His Holy Spirit into you until first you had been made holy. The Holy Spirit is not given to make you holy, but because God reckons you as holy through your life in His Holy Son.

You are being changed into God's likeness from one degree of glory to another; and this is the work of the Holy Spirit in your life. How can you be regarded as holy and yet still need to be changed to be more like Him? Because Jesus Christ is your holiness. He places His Holy Spirit within you to enable you to be more and more like Him in your daily living, in your performance. Through the influence of the Holy Spirit working within you, God's purpose is that your performance will match your position more closely.

If it were not true that your acceptance depended on the work of Jesus, you would be left in legalistic bondage. At what point would you become acceptable? What would be the standard of holiness and righteousness acceptable to God? The only standard acceptable to Him is perfection, and you would have no hope of attaining that standard by your efforts. If you still had to work to win acceptance you would be condemned to a life of striving.

You can only be considered perfect in God's sight because of your position in the Perfect One. You can only live in righteousness and holiness because you are in Christ, who is your righteousness and holiness. You may fail at times to live up to your high calling, but He never fails! And your standing before God depends ultimately on His performance, not your own!

That does not mean that your performance is irrelevant; for the more your performance matches your position in Christ, the more effective you are as His witness and the more He is able to use you for His glory. His life will flow more freely out of you to others.

Not only is Christ the One who redeemed you, purchasing you for God with His own life and blood, but He is also your redemption! You stay redeemed because you are in Him. You belong and always will belong to God's eternal Kingdom because you are in Him. None shall snatch you from His hand.

In all these truths you see what a wonderful salvation God has secured for you. You see that all of this depends completely on His mercy. **By His mercy you are forgiven, you are accepted in Christ, clothed with Him. By His mercy, Jesus Christ is your righteousness, holiness and redemption. By His mercy Jesus suffered the death penalty you deserve and by God's great mercy you are alive in Christ!**

Even when we fail to live up to this wonderful position we have in Christ, God maintains His mercy towards us by forgiving and restoring us. What a God of mercy! No wonder the Psalmist says that He is 'slow to anger and rich in love. The Lord is good to all; he has compassion on all he has made' (Ps. 145:8–9).

The teaching of our position in Christ is a very important emphasis in the New Testament, especially in Paul's letters. It has always been an important aspect of the teaching at Kingdom Faith, in both the church and the Bible College.

Only when you are secure in your knowledge of your place in Christ are you able to deal successfully with the lies and accusations Satan throws at you. He cannot take you out of Christ, he cannot undo the work that Jesus has done for you. However, he will try to prevent you from living in the good of your position in Christ. He continually reminds you of your failures so that your attention is diverted away from Jesus and the position you have in Him, and on to yourself. The enemy wants you to think of yourself as an unrighteous failure, not as one totally accepted by God and clothed with Jesus's righteousness! He wants you to feel guilty and weighed down by sin, instead of rejoicing in your place in Christ Jesus.

There is no revival without faith in the truth of Jesus and all He has done for us. So the more God continued the process of leading us into revival, the more these truths gripped our hearts and lives. Again and again the Holy Spirit brought the relevant scriptures to us, showing us that our minds needed to be renewed, to be set free from thinking that centred on 'self', and filled with revelation of the truth of God's Word.

Many realised that they had spent years, even as Christians, living in false condemnation instead of victory, simply because they had listened to the lying accusations of the evil one. They could take the shield of faith and quench all these fiery arrows. They could take up the sword of the Spirit, which is the Word of God, and boldly proclaim the truth about themselves: **'Jesus is my righteousness. I am completely accepted by God because I am in Him!'**

Sin and failure are to be confessed, forgiven and forgotten! It is for freedom Christ has set us free!

10

By His Grace

The nation needs a revelation of God's mercy. The idea of a move of the Spirit that would bring such a revelation of mercy to multitudes was a great incentive to persevere in our prayer for revival. Such a move of God would have to be a work of His grace.

His mercy and grace are closely related and yet distinctive. Following this fresh revelation of His mercy, God now began to speak to us about His grace. Because of His mercy God does not treat us in the way we deserve. Of ourselves, we deserve nothing; but He deals with us as those who are fully accepted in His Son, Jesus.

Grace is usually defined as 'the free, unmerited favour of God'. We deserve nothing; but He chooses to give us everything, the fullness of His life. **Through grace God gives everything to those who deserve nothing!**

Mercy is the entrance into God's grace. Because He has been merciful to you, accepting you in Jesus, you can expect Him to be gracious to you! He is merciful by nature; He is also gracious by nature. If it were not for His grace we could receive nothing from Him.

Because we are totally dependent on Jesus for our acceptance, we have no claim on God through anything we have accomplished. We can never suggest that we deserve His gifts, or that in any way we could earn them. **Everything we receive from Him is a work of His grace**. He is ready to be exceedingly gracious to us so that He can reproduce His graciousness in us;

> And God is able to make all grace abound to you, so that in all things at all times, having all that you need, you will abound in every good work. (2 Cor. 9:8)

There are several important lessons we are to learn from this one verse:

1. **God is able to do anything He chooses because He is Almighty. He is gracious because He chooses to be gracious; and there is no limit to His graciousness, to what He is able and willing to give to us, although we deserve nothing!**
2. **It is God who makes all grace abound to you.** This is His purpose. He wants *all* His gifts to be poured into your life, so that you experience His abundance. He wants you to know His abundant generosity.
3. **He wants His grace to be manifested to you in all things.** This must mean in all circumstances of your life. Clearly this is not some spiritual cliché. God wants to supply all *things* that you need; material as well as spiritual supply!
4. **He wants to provide for you at all times.** Again this must mean in every situation, for there cannot be a moment in time when God does not want to give to you by His grace.
5. **God's purpose is that you will have 'all that you need'.** He never wants to leave you in need. His grace is sufficient to meet every need.
6. Why should God want to lavish so much generosity on to you? So that **'you will abound in every good work'.** He knows you cannot give what you have not first received, and the more you receive, the more you will have to give. The more you are a recipient of His grace, the more gracious you can be! The more like Him you will be in the way in which you give to others!

Are there any conditions to receiving such grace from God? You can never earn or deserve anything from Him. You cannot receive by grace anything that you have earned on merit or deserve. However, it is clear from the scriptures that three things enable you to receive what God wants to give you.

First, you need to ask. Jesus Himself makes this clear in His teaching. You are to ask the Father in prayer for whatever you need and He will give it to you. 'Ask and you will receive . . . Everyone who asks receives.'

Second, you need to have faith when you ask. Just as you need to believe in God's mercy, in His willingness to forgive and accept you, so you need to believe in His willingness to give graciously to you, although you deserve nothing! This is easier said than done, because most people think they should deserve something before they can expect to receive it. If God waited until you deserved to receive from Him, He would never give you anything!

To believe in God's grace is to say: **'I believe God will give to me, although I deserve nothing.'**

Third, it is in giving that you are able to receive. This does not mean you earn God's blessings by giving. No, the giving puts you in the spiritual condition in which you are able to receive what God wants to give to you. He always wants to be gracious; He is poised, ready to give to you. The point at which He releases a gift or an answer to prayer is often the point at which you give first. Paul says:

> Whoever sows sparingly will also reap sparingly, and whoever sows generously will also reap generously. (2 Cor. 9:6)

This is in line with what we read elsewhere, that we reap what we sow (Gal. 6:8). The measure we give, says Jesus, is the measure we receive in return (Matt. 7:2).

Of course, what God gives to us far outweighs anything we can give. So we are not talking about earning or deserving

His gifts, but of an attitude, a disposition of the heart. It is in giving that we receive.

Paul also indicates that God loves a cheerful giver, one who gives willingly and freely – as He gives! He is not blessed when we give begrudgingly or simply as an attempt to manipulate Him into doing something for us. He quickly sees through such motives!

The act of cheerful, generous giving opens our hearts to be able to receive what God wants to give us. It is not difficult to see the evidence for this truth.

God wanted to save you by His grace, to forgive your sins and give you the gift of eternal life. When did you receive that salvation? Not until you first gave yourself willingly to Him, when you turned to Him in repentance and faith. Salvation was awaiting you and yet had to be appropriated. When you turned to Him, He lavished His mercy upon you, forgiving your sins, and by His grace gave you new birth, giving you the gift of eternal life, making you a co-heir with Christ.

You see the same principle at work in the major events of your Christian life. When did God baptise you in the Holy Spirit, or give you fresh anointing? When you recognised your need, turned to Him in faith, giving yourself afresh to Him and thereby making yourself available to receive what He wanted to give you.

It is not surprising that God wants to lavish such grace upon you for this was the first disciples' experience of Jesus. John speaks of Jesus being the Word of God that came to live among us. He gives us a series of great theological truths about Him:

> The Word became flesh and made his dwelling among us. We have seen his glory, the glory of the One and Only, who came from the Father, full of grace and truth. (John 1:14)

Jesus came from heaven full of grace. Now 'full' means there is no room for anything that is a contradiction to grace. He was *full* of grace. And as He came to show us what the Father is like, we can see that **God's nature and disposition is to be full of grace towards us.** John adds this word of testimony:

> From the fullness of his grace we have all received one blessing after another. (John 1:16)

This verse teaches us:

1 **Being full of grace had many practical results in Jesus's ministry.**
2 **All His followers, not only John, received the benefits of this grace.**
3 **Those benefits meant they received one blessing after another.**

This is how God wants His grace to operate in your life, so that you receive through Jesus blessing upon blessing! **Because you are a child of His grace, you are to receive blessing after blessing after blessing after blessing!**

Does this seem selfish? Not at all! You cannot accuse God of being over-generous; it is He who chooses to bless. You cannot make Him give what He does not want to give. And you can only give to others what you have first received. So the more you trust in God's grace, the more blessings you receive, and the greater blessing you can be to others. John continues:

> For the law was given through Moses; grace and truth came through Jesus Christ. (v. 17)

God did not lack grace before He sent Jesus. If He had not been gracious He would not have sent His Son! There are many Old Testament scriptures which speak of God's graciousness. For example:

> But you are a forgiving God, gracious and compassionate, slow to anger and abounding in love. (Neh. 9:17)

> The Lord is gracious and compassionate. (Ps. 111:4)

> The Lord is gracious and righteous; our God is full of compassion. (Ps. 116:5)

And when he prays, David appeals to God's graciousness:

> Be gracious to me according to your promise. (Ps. 119:58)

Isaiah assured the people:

> Yet the Lord longs to be gracious to you; he rises to show you compassion. (Isa. 30:18)

And he prays:

> O Lord, be gracious to us; we long for you. Be our strength every morning, our salvation in time of distress. (Isa. 33:2)

So God did not suddenly become gracious when Jesus came. He inaugurated a new covenant of God's grace; a new relationship was made possible in which we could receive His abundance freely.

Notice how often, in these Old Testament verses quoted above, God's compassion or mercy is mentioned in connection with His grace – and this is only a selection of verses where this is the case. This reinforces what was said before: His mercy is the entrance to His grace. **He draws you by His mercy into a new relationship with Himself through Jesus Christ, so that He can then lavish His blessings on you in the gracious way He desires.**

Why should He want to bless you in this way? Because He

loves you. And when you love someone you want to give to that person, because you are concerned about him and do not want to see him in need.

God even shows grace to the wicked (Isa. 26:10). Otherwise all those outside His covenant of grace could have nothing, but would suffer the deprivation of the judgement they deserve from Him. Those who are part of the new covenant, sealed by the blood of Jesus, can expect God's graciousness. He wants them to believe in His generosity, His desire and willingness to give to them because He loves them!

God gives us grace to enable us to fulfil His Kingdom purposes. During the period concerned by the Acts of the Apostles, **'much grace was upon them all'** (Acts 4:33).

Stephen did great wonders and miraculous signs among the people because he was a man **'full of God's grace and power'** (Acts 6:8).

When Barnabas arrived at Antioch, he saw **'the evidence of the grace of God'** (Acts 11:23). He saw the way they were being blessed and knew that God was with them.

Paul and Barnabas urged the people **'to continue in the grace of God'** (Acts 13:43). At Iconium they spoke 'boldly for the Lord, **who confirmed the message of his grace** by enabling them to do miraculous signs and wonders' (Acts 14:3).

Grace was at the very heart of their gospel and of their experience of the way in which God worked:

> We believe **it is through the grace of our Lord Jesus that we are saved**. (Acts 15:11)

Because this was the substance of the apostles' preaching and teaching, Paul said:

> I consider my life worth nothing to me, if only I may finish the race and complete the task the Lord Jesus has given me – **the task of testifying to the gospel of God's grace**. (Acts 20:24)

Not surprisingly, therefore, he speaks often of God's grace in his epistles, and this with good reason. Because he had persecuted the Church before his conversion, being responsible for the death and imprisonment of many Christians, Paul considered himself to be the chief of sinners. And yet God had not dealt with him as he deserved. Instead of judging him, the Lord had graciously called him, met with him, forgiven him, healed him, filled him with the Holy Spirit and given him this amazing ministry as the great apostle to the Gentile nations.

And so, understandably, Paul could never lose sight of God's grace, and urged others to live in a continual revelation of that grace. And when he spoke of this grace that God has for all His children, he frequently used lavish terms:

> In him we have redemption through his blood, the forgiveness of sins, **in accordance with the riches of God's grace that he lavished on us** with all wisdom and understanding. (Eph. 1:7–8)

This theme of God's grace was central to the apostles' presentation of the gospel.

1 **We are justified**, freely made righteous and acceptable before God, **by the grace revealed through Jesus Christ**. (Rom. 3:24)
2 By our faith in Jesus, **we now stand in God's grace**. (Rom. 5:2)
3 **We can receive the blessings of God's grace** only because of the grace revealed in Jesus. (Rom. 5:15)
4 Because **we have received God's abundant provision of grace** and His gift of righteousness, we are able to reign in life through Jesus Christ (Rom. 5:21). That means we are to be victors, not victims!
5 We are no longer under law, trying to please God by obedience to a written code. **Now we are under grace**, accepted because we are in Christ and recipients of every

blessing God makes available through Him. Because we are no longer under law, we are no longer in bondage to sin! (Rom. 6:14)

6 **We are called and chosen by grace**, not according to anything we have done (Rom. 11:5–6).

7 **The gifts we receive from God are the evidence of His grace** (Rom. 12:6).

8 **God manifested His grace through Jesus**, 'that though he was rich, yet for your sakes he became poor, **so that you through his poverty might become rich**' (2 Cor. 8:9).

9 Because of the generosity of their giving, Paul speaks to the Corinthians of: **'the surpassing grace God has given you'** (2 Cor. 9:14).

10 **Paul recognises his complete dependence on God's grace** to fulfil his ministry and to communicate the gospel effectively (Rom. 15:15; 1 Cor. 3:10, 15:10; 2 Cor. 1:12; Eph. 3:7–8).

11 He urges his readers **not to receive God's grace in vain** (2 Cor. 6:1). Having tasted His grace they are not to return to trying to please Him through their works.

12 The Lord taught Paul personally, '**My grace is sufficient for you**, for my power is made perfect in weakness' (2 Cor. 12:9). No matter what the situation, God could supply whatever Paul needed. When he felt weak at the greatness of the tasks before him, this was encouragement to trust in God's power which was his, and every believer's, through God's grace.

13 He was astonished that having tasted God's grace, the Galatians so quickly deserted **'the one who called you by the grace of Christ'** by turning to a different gospel (Gal. 1:6).

14 **Paul refused to set aside the grace of God,** 'for if righteousness could be gained through the law, Christ died for nothing!' (Gal. 2:21).

15 To try to continue in God's acceptance through works rather than faith in His grace is to be alienated from Christ; 'to have fallen away from grace' (Gal. 5:4). **The**

only way in which we can relate to God through our life in Christ is by grace.

16 Paul speaks of **God's 'glorious grace, which he has freely given us in the One he loves'** (Eph. 1:6). What is the point in trying to earn or win God's favour, when He has freely given us His acceptance in Jesus? To Paul fleshly striving seems ludicrous, an evidence of unbelief and an affront to God who has given us so much in Jesus.

17 **The whole work of redemption is a gift of God's grace.** He has been merciful to us so that we can enjoy a wonderful relationship of grace with Him (Eph. 1:7).

18 God wants to demonstrate to the world **'the incomparable riches of his grace, expressed in his kindness to us in Christ Jesus'** (Eph. 2:7). This is impossible if we are trying to please Him through religious laws or loyalty to denominational traditions.

19 **'For it is by grace you have been saved, through faith – and this is not from yourselves, it is the gift of God – not by works, so that no one can boast'** (Eph. 2:8–9).

20 The gospel is spread by understanding **'God's grace in all its truth'** (Col. 1:6).

21 **God can only be glorified in us as believers 'according to the grace of our God and the Lord Jesus Christ'** (2 Thess. 1:12).

22 **By His grace God has given us eternal encouragement and good hope** (2 Thess. 2:16).

23 Paul testifies: **'The grace of our Lord was poured out on me abundantly,** along with the faith and love that are in Christ Jesus' (1 Tim. 1:14).

24 God 'has saved us and called us to a holy life – not because of anything we have done but because of his own purpose and grace. **This grace was given us in Christ Jesus** before the beginning of time' (2 Tim. 1:9). This proves to us that God did not suddenly become gracious. He decided before time began to be gracious to us in Jesus. You receive that grace when you turn to Him in faith. Paul cannot understand anybody being so foolish as to

return to religious law and try to please God through their works and effort, once they have experienced that God graciously gives us all things in Christ!

25 **By God's grace, Jesus tasted death for everyone** (Heb. 2:9). To deny or desert that grace is a denial of Christ Himself.

26 **We approach God's throne of grace, and there we receive 'mercy and find grace to help us in our time of need'** (Heb. 4:16).

27 **Peter urges us to set our hope 'fully on the grace to be given you when Jesus Christ is revealed'** (1 Pet. 1:13). We have received God's grace; daily we receive His grace as we live out our lives in Christ; and there is still more of His grace for us to receive when Jesus comes again!

28 We are faithfully to administer to others, **'God's grace in its various forms'**. God blesses us graciously in many different ways that we may administer the benefits of His grace to others (1 Pet. 4:10).

29 'God opposes the proud but **gives grace to the humble**' (1 Pet. 5:5).

30 **He is 'the God of all grace'** (1 Pet. 5:10).

31 Peter urges his readers to **stand fast in God's grace** (1 Pet. 5:12).

32 We are to **'grow in the grace and knowledge of our Lord and Saviour Jesus Christ'** (2 Pet. 3:18).

33 **'Grace and peace be yours in *abundance* through the knowledge of God and of Jesus our Lord'** (2 Pet. 1:2).

34 The apostles begin and end their letters with greetings centred on God's grace. They perceive that **everything we receive from God, from first to last, is the work of His grace.** And they mean their readers to be aware constantly of that grace! Paul's typical opening greeting is: 'Grace and peace to you from God our Father and the Lord Jesus Christ' (1 Cor. 1:3). And he usually closes his letters by saying: 'The grace of the Lord Jesus be with you' (1 Cor. 16:23). And John writes: 'Grace, mercy and peace from God the Father and from Jesus Christ, the

Father's Son, will be with us in truth and love' (2 John 3). And the very last verse of scripture reads: 'The grace of the Lord Jesus be with God's people. Amen.'

So we cannot escape the centrality of grace in the teaching of the New Testament. And yet, even in those early days of the Church, there is already the temptation to desert grace and return to works. Instead of living by faith in what God has graciously done and given in Christ, there was the temptation to return to law. Sadly, these same failings have dogged the Church throughout history and are all too predominant today!

We are not only to preach grace but are to live by God's grace. He is willing to give bountifully in every way in which we need to receive from Him. It is clear that we cannot preach grace on the one hand and live by law or tradition on the other, allowing things that are a contradiction to grace, whether at a personal or corporate level in the Church.

As the Lord spoke to us about His grace, our sense of expectancy was raised. We knew He was leading us into the full blessing of revival, that when this finally came it would be like receiving a gracious gift from Him. We had done all we could do from the human side: praying, believing, seeking Him.

And yet at the same time we were being further challenged. How far did we really trust in His willingness to be gracious to us at a personal level as well as corporately?

A significant change of attitude took place. We began to realise that He wanted to give us revival far more than we wanted to receive it! In His wisdom, He was preparing the ground and awaiting His appointed time.

11

The Galatian Lesson: Grace, Not Law!

Everything God gives is a work of His grace – even revival!

Most at Kingdom Faith had never experienced revival. As God moved upon us again and again by His Spirit, there was always the question: 'Is this it?' The few of us who had experienced revival had to say: 'No, this is not revival yet, but we are closer. Keep persevering, keep praying and waiting. God will fulfil His promise.' We knew God would not have called us to be a revival church unless it was His intention to lead us into revival, to impart this gracious gift to us.

Paul had led a strict religious life as a Pharisee and had been entrusted by the Jewish authorities with the commission to persecute the followers of Jesus Christ. However, his personal encounter with Jesus on the road to Damascus began a process in which Paul came to understand that 'a man is not justified by observing the law, but by faith in Jesus Christ'. He was delivered from a life of seeking to please God by the strict observance of religious duties and holding on to the traditions of his forefathers. He discovered that **a person can only be made acceptable in God's sight through faith in what Jesus has done for him**. A believer's acceptance is in Christ. He taught this wherever he went: that **people can only be saved by faith in God's work of grace**.

> So we, too, have put our faith in Christ Jesus that we may be justified by faith in Christ and not by observing the

> law, because by observing the law no one will be justified. (Gal. 2:16)

To put your faith in Jesus means that you believe that when He died you died with Him. Your old life has passed away; you are born again and Christ comes to live in you. You die to the whole idea of trying to please God by what you do, and realise you are only pleasing to Him because of what He has done for you in Jesus.

> I died to the law so that I might live for God. I have been crucified with Christ and I no longer live, but Christ lives in me. (Gal. 2:19–20)

Far from believing this, many Christians try to please God by their own works, through their religious practices and traditions. Paul is emphatic: that is impossible! Nobody has ever succeeded in pleasing God in that way.

It is not only a question of believing in God's grace at the outset of the Christian life. The believer is to continue to live in His grace. God's graciousness is to be a continual process in his life. It is wrong to think that we receive a work of God's grace at the outset of our Christian lives, but are then expected to return to our religious practices and traditions in order to please God. We are not delivered from law, taken into God's grace, only to return to law again!

This was the mistake made by those to whom Paul writes the Galatian epistle, and he cannot believe they could be so stupid.

> You foolish Galatians! Who has bewitched you? (Gal. 3:1)

That is very strong language and Paul is obviously angry and amazed at their foolishness. It seems that they must have come under the influence of some evil spell. Having tasted

God's grace, he cannot understand why they should return to the thinking that suggests they could please God and be acceptable to Him through their own religious effort. The only way to please God is to live by faith in Jesus Christ:

> The life I live in the body, I live by faith in the Son of God, who loved me and gave himself for me. (Gal. 2:20)

Paul is furious with the Galatians because they have listened to legalistic preachers who followed him around. Although purporting to belong to Christ these men preached a travesty of the gospel. They believed that even new Gentile converts had to become 'Jews' to be properly saved by submitting to the written, legalistic code and the Jewish traditions. They also taught that those Jews who came to faith in Jesus were still to be bound by those laws and traditions. Paul points out that this denies the work of the cross and sets aside the work of grace that God has accomplished for us:

> I do not set aside the grace of God, for if righteousness could be gained through the law, Christ died for nothing! (Gal. 2:21)

Sadly all this has its modern counterparts. There are those within some churches who scoff at the idea of being saved by God's grace, and teach that we will only be judged by our works. This is no gospel at all. In such teaching sin is given very little emphasis and faith in the cross at a personal level scarcely exists.

But there are many others who are deceived by a more subtle doctrine, and this was the failing of those in Galatia. This suggests that only by coming to personal repentance and faith in Jesus Christ, crucified and risen from the dead, is salvation possible. But then it is taught that to please God you must prove faithful to your denominational practices and traditions. To be acceptable you must obey their laws and rules.

Paul sees this as a travesty of the gospel because it begins with faith in God's grace, but then sets that grace aside! He says:

> Before your very eyes Jesus Christ was clearly portrayed as crucified. (Gal. 3:1)

He had taught them that their acceptance for all time and eternity was dependent on the mercy and grace of God revealed on the cross, not through any efforts of their own. They could never have a righteousness of their own, but only that which is by faith in Jesus. The Christian life is a matter of faith in God's grace from beginning to end.

The Christian begins by faith in Jesus, continues in faith and will go to glory believing. This is because God has extended His grace to him, continues to extend His grace and will always be gracious to the believer.

All that Jesus has done for the individual believer has eternal significance. **If Christ is my righteousness, He will always be my righteousness, throughout my life on earth and for all eternity**. I will never reach the point at which I do not need Him to be my righteousness. I cannot stand before God, even for a moment, confident because of my works, of what I have done or accomplished, no matter how much God has used me. I can only stand confident in His presence because I am clothed with Christ; He is my righteousness, holiness and redemption!

To suggest that my works matter in the whole business of my acceptance before God is to suggest that what Jesus has done for me is somehow incomplete, inadequate or temporary, and has to be completed by what I do myself: grace followed by my works, faith followed by my own striving and efforts.

Paul is absolutely clear: this is *not* the gospel. There is no good news in this; to be saved I would be dependent on myself, at least in part, if this was the case.

Those who preached such nonsense did not like Paul's

continual emphasis on grace. They thought that it suggested to people that it did not matter how they lived once they believed they were saved. Anybody reading Paul's writings will see clearly that he did not believe or teach that. He was clear that the work of salvation was God's work and His alone. It was a work of sheer grace on His part and could never be attained through anything we could do. We can only trust in this work of His grace.

The way we live, however, is also of great importance. **We walk in righteousness, holiness and obedience, not to be saved but because by God's grace we have been saved**. The more you appreciate that this work of salvation is fully completed and is the evidence of God's amazing love for you, the more readily you will desire to obey Him.

To think that you have to please God by your performance easily leads not only to much striving, but also to a hard-hearted, cold, evangelical self-righteousness in which it is difficult to sense the graciousness of God, His mercy and love, His loving care and acceptance. Instead, judgemental and critical attitudes are all too common and inspire fear of men rather than love for God.

Unfortunately, many have suffered under preaching where there is more emphasis on sin and failure than on God's grace and love; and have suffered in legalistic congregations where there is little freedom of the Holy Spirit, because the leadership is authoritarian. Paul asks the Galatians.

> Did you receive the Spirit by observing the law, or by believing what you heard? (Gal. 3:2)

The construction of the Greek indicates that the answer to the question can only be 'by believing what we heard!' Paul continues:

> Are you so foolish? After beginning with the Spirit, are you now trying to attain your goal by human effort? (Gal. 3:3)

He then poses a further question:

> Does God give you his Spirit and work miracles among you because you observe the law, or because you believe what you heard? (Gal. 3:5)

Again there can only be one answer to the question: 'by believing what we heard!' In these verses Paul has made these important points:

1 At the beginning of their Christian lives, they received the Holy Spirit **because they believed the gospel of God's grace** that Paul preached to them.
2 God continued to pour out His Spirit on them and they saw miracles happening **because they believed what they had heard through God's Word**.
3 Now the Galatians have deserted the word Paul preached, and so have wandered from the truth! As a result they have returned to law and bondage, and have lost their freedom. They no longer experience the moving of God's Spirit and His miracles as they did **when they believed the revelation of all that God had done for them on the cross**.

In the next part of the letter Paul expands on the theme that 'the righteous will live by faith' (3:11). All God's promises can only be appropriated through faith. The law was only given by God 'to lead us to Christ that we might be justified by faith. Now that faith has come, we are no longer under the supervision of the law' (3:24–25).

By faith the Galatians have become sons of God, they have been baptised into Christ and have clothed themselves with Him.

> You are all sons of God through faith in Christ Jesus, for all of you who were baptised into Christ have clothed yourselves with Christ. (3:26–27)

Notice that Paul says they clothe themselves with Christ. This is the result of faith, to put on Christ day by day. To live in Him. To live in Christ is to live as a son of God, to relate to Him as your Father. You can think as a son of God, speak as a son of God, act as a son of God – in faith, in love, with true spiritual authority and power.

To live as a son is to recognise that you are a son and always will be, irrespective of what you do. In the parable Jesus taught, the prodigal remained a son, even though he deserted his father and wasted his inheritance. When he returned home, his father accepted him as a son and treated him as such, not as one of the servants.

The climax of this epistle is a great cry from Paul's heart:

> It is for freedom that Christ has set us free. (Gal. 5:1)

He does not say the believers will be set free. **They have already been set free – from sin, from bondage to religious law, from traditions, from the enemy.** Therefore he tells them:

> Stand firm, then, and do not let yourselves be burdened again by a yoke of slavery. (Gal. 5:1)

They are no longer yoked to legalistic religion and tradition. They are yoked to Christ.

> The only thing that counts is faith expressing itself through love. (Gal. 5:6)

Having begun with faith they now need to return to a position of faith:

> You were running a good race. Who cut in on you and kept you from obeying the truth? (Gal. 5:7)

He warns that 'a little yeast works through the whole batch of dough' (5:9). They need to stand against this other teaching with its dependence on law and works. A little unbelief in what Jesus has done and the standing given to believers in Him will rapidly affect all their attitudes, and will seep insidiously into every area of the believer's life.

Paul understands that preaching of the total victory and provision of the cross is an offence to many; nevertheless, it is the truth. And, as Jesus made clear, **only the truth sets people free.** So he urges his readers to return to faith in the truth:

> You, my brothers, were called to be free. (Gal. 5:13)

However, he warns against thinking that this means they can be careless about the way they live:

> But do not use your freedom to indulge the sinful nature [the flesh]; rather, serve one another in love. (Gal. 5:13)

Paul knows that to fight the flesh only stirs up the flesh:

> So I say, live by the Spirit, and you will not gratify the desires of the sinful nature [the flesh]. (5:16)

The final part of this letter is about walking in the Spirit, bearing the fruit of the Spirit. He points out that: 'Those who belong to Christ Jesus have crucified the sinful nature with its passions and desires' (5:24). They have died with Christ and need no longer be bound by the flesh. They are free to live in the Spirit and express the life of Christ who lives in them. Not surprisingly Paul closes the letter by saying:

> May I never boast except in the cross of our Lord Jesus Christ, through which the world has been crucified to me, and I to the world. (Gal. 6:14)

The believer cannot put himself to death. He needs that revelation of faith in his heart whereby he knows that when

Christ died, he died with Him; that he has now been raised to a new life.

I once had a vision from God that helped me to appreciate that I really am dead and buried with Christ and have been raised to a new life in Him.

At the time we were experiencing a powerful move of God's Spirit in the meeting. The Lord told me to lie on the floor on my back while many others all around me were meeting with God. I thought that perhaps the Lord wanted me to be still, to rest in Him and receive from Him.

To my astonishment as I lay there, I saw myself in my coffin. There was no fear, only a deep sense of peace. I saw the lid put on the coffin and watched it being lowered into the grave and the grave then being filled in. It was a strange experience because it was as if I were at the same time in the coffin and yet able to watch what was happening.

Then I saw something difficult to describe. I saw myself sit up in the coffin and rise up through the lid, the earth, and stand on top of the grave. I was in my body, but it had the properties of a risen body like that of Jesus which enabled Him to go through walls and appear at different localities; and yet could tell Thomas to put his hand into His wounds. This is not to suggest that my physical resurrection has already taken place, but God was showing me that I have been raised to a new life.

As I stood on the grave, Jesus stood there to greet me: 'That wasn't so bad, was it?' was all He said. But it was enough!

We somehow fear to face the fact of our death in Christ, even though it is a historical event that has already taken place. We imagine we can put off this moment of death, of surrender, when it has already happened. **The sooner you appreciate that you have been crucified with Christ, the sooner you will be able to rise up in faith and walk through life with Jesus in the power of the Holy Spirit.**

As believers, we are dead men and women raised to a new life in Christ. Now a dead man can be nothing except dead, and he can possess nothing either. So if you reckon yourself as dead you cannot seek acceptance of yourself! Neither can you have any righteousness or virtue of your own. All your works apart from Christ are worthless. You have no life or identity apart from Him. There is no point, therefore, in seeking ministry or healing for what has been consigned to death.

You are raised to a new life in Christ. Your body is now a temple of His living presence. In this new life, He is your righteousness. You are totally accepted by God because you are in Him. He is your holiness and your redemption. You can live out the rest of your life in Him. It is for this reason that Jesus said to the disciples:

> Remain in me, and I will remain in you. (John 15:4)

The Greek word translated 'remain' is in a continuous tense and is sometimes translated 'abide'. It means literally: 'Go on continually living in me'. Continue to live where God has placed you: in Christ Jesus. He is your life and in Him you are already made complete! And as you continue to live in Him and allow the truth of God's Word to live in you, you have this wonderful promise from Jesus:

> If you remain in me and my words remain in you, ask whatever you wish, and it will be given you. (John 15:7)

That is the fruit of the ongoing relationship of faith in Jesus, of your life in Him! That is far better than returning to religious attitudes, trying to please God by your efforts and good works. In your flesh, your self-life, there is nothing good, according to Jesus. Apart from Him you can do nothing.

In Christ you have everything. Through God's abundant grace in all things at all times, you can have all that you need so that you will abound in every good work! You can walk in the Spirit and you will not gratify the desires of the flesh.

You can rise up in faith, confident that God considers you His and that you are righteous, holy, forgiven and accepted, simply because He has placed you in His Son, Jesus. He is your life!

For nearly three years we had sought God to meet with us in revival power. He had blessed and anointed us in many ways. Every time of prayer, every week that was set aside to seek Him, was important and proved to be worth while. The times of preparation were important because these made us ready to receive His grace. When He sowed the mustard seed of multiplication, it would need to fall into good soil that would be productive.

The Lord gave us an illustration to explain the process through which He was taking us. We were climbing a mountain, much as the three disciples had to climb the high mountain of Transfiguration with Jesus. The climb would be worth while, for revival lay at the summit.

And this would bring us a much greater revelation of Jesus Himself. Every time of prayer and of seeking God enabled us to make progress up the mountain.

For the most part the progress was steady. The weeks we set aside for revival meetings enabled us to rise to new heights. But no matter how high we climbed, the final stage was a sheer precipice that was unscalable. Only the Lord Himself could reach down, raise us up and place us on the summit.

And this He has graciously done!

12

God is Love

During previous times of revival I had experienced, there had been a great outpouring of God's love upon us as a people. We came to know and understand His love more fully, and this deeply affected our relationships with one another. God's love for us overflowed in an increased love for each other.

'God is love' (1 John 4:8). His love is not a sentimental emotion; but a love that is unchanging, strong and reliable, yet tender. As with the other characteristics of His Father's nature, Jesus revealed this love within the limitations of a human body. He showed us what it means to love with God's love – how to love the Father, other believers, our neighbours, and even ourselves, in the sense of having self-acceptance because we are fully accepted by God.

Because He is eternally the same, God has always been love. So before He showed His love for us in the incarnation of Jesus, He revealed His love to His people, Israel. David said: 'Your love, O Lord, reaches to the heavens' (Ps. 36:5). He could affirm: 'I trust in your unfailing love; my heart rejoices in your salvation' (Ps. 13:5). 'For great is your love towards me; you have delivered me from the depths of the grave' (Ps. 86:13). He is the Lord who is 'a compassionate and gracious God, slow to anger, abounding in love and faithfulness' (Ps. 86:15).

God's love and faithfulness belong together. **His love is steadfast, sure and certain; it does not change with**

circumstances or emotion, and is in no way dependent on how others respond to that love.

> Give thanks to the Lord, for he is good; his love endures for ever. (Ps. 107:1)

Even though His people sometimes stray from His ways, when they cry out to the Lord He delivers them out of their need. David knew the Lord's love; so when he sinned grievously he prayed:

> Have mercy on me, O God, according to your unfailing love; according to your great compassion blot out my transgressions. (Ps. 51:1)

God's love is not only closely related to His faithfulness, but also to His mercy. As we have seen, this is the first way in which He reveals His love to His people. On this occasion David had gone so far away from the Lord's purposes, he knew he needed a fresh taste of mercy that would lead him into a fresh revelation of God's love for him. He could later say:

> Praise be to God, who has not rejected my prayer or withheld his love from me! (Ps. 66:20)

And He never wants to withhold His love from you!

By definition, God cannot do anything imperfectly. Because He loves you, He loves you perfectly. And you cannot improve on the perfect! So the person reading these words now is loved by God as much as any other person in all of creation.

How much you know that love, trust in that love and enjoy a loving relationship with the One who loves you, is another matter. But God did not start to love you the moment you began to love Him. He always loved you and you could only belong to Him now because of that love. **You can only love because He first loved you**! (1 Jn. 4:19)

He expressed that love in sending Jesus to die for your sins, to take you to the cross so that you could die with Him and be raised to a new life in Him. He guaranteed His eternal love for you by giving you eternal life and filling you with the gift of His Holy Spirit. And He wants to have a daily relationship with you in which you walk together with Him in love:

> I have loved you with an everlasting love; I have drawn you with loving-kindness. (Jer. 31:3)

Even though His people were so often disobedient God said:

> I led them with cords of human kindness, with ties of love; I lifted the yoke from their neck and bent down to feed them. (Hos. 11:4)

As with His mercy and grace, so God's love leads Him to positive action. He expresses His mercy in forgiving His people and reconciling them to Himself. He expresses His grace in giving us His salvation, His everything, although we deserve nothing. And He expresses His love supremely in sending His Son to meet every need, to die for us and to raise us to a new life in Him.

God's love moves Him to action. He is not like those who affirm that they love others but do not lift a finger to help them! When Jesus came in human flesh He demonstrated that He was totally secure in the Father's love for Him. When He was baptised at the beginning of His ministry, a voice from heaven said, 'This is my Son, whom I love; with him I am well pleased' (Matt 3:17).

At His transfiguration, when three of the disciples saw His body glorified, a voice from the cloud said, 'This is my Son, whom I love; with him I am well pleased. Listen to him!' (Matt 17:5)

We see that He lived in the security of that love, in such a close relationship with His Father, that He could say: 'Anyone who has seen me has seen the Father' (John 14:9).

Jesus revealed God's love in His teaching, but above all in the cross.

> Jesus knew that the time had come for him to leave this world and go to the Father. Having loved his own who were in the world, he now showed them the full extent of his love. (John 13:1)

Because of His great love for us, God has had mercy on us; He has forgiven us instead of judging us; accepted us instead of condemning us, and has given us eternal life instead of eternal death.

All we can do is to believe what He has done for us in His love and live in the good of that. This does not lead us to a life of passive inactivity. Quite the opposite. Anyone who truly knows God's love will be very active in declaring that love to others, not only in words but in deeds. Love for God will be expressed in loving others! **He reveals His love to us and then places that love in us by the Holy Spirit, to enable us to love Him and others in His name.** Jesus prayed:

> I have made you known to them, and will continue to make you known in order that the love you have for me may be in them and that I myself may be in them. (John 17:26)

Think of that: as a believer, **God's own love for Jesus has been placed in you.** You can love Him with the love that God has given you. And if you love Jesus you will obey His commands.

> If anyone loves me, he will obey my teaching. My Father will love him, and we will come to him and make our home with him. (John 14:23)

Because He loved the Father, Jesus obeyed Him, even to the point of death:

> The world must learn that I love the Father and that I do exactly what my Father has commanded me. (John 14:31)

For me, these words that Jesus says to His disciples are among the most amazing in scripture:

> **As the Father has loved me, so have I loved you. Now remain in my love.** (John 15:9)

When you receive this as personal revelation, you realise that Jesus loves you in exactly the same way the Father loved Him: perfectly! **Yes, you are loved perfectly by Jesus!** Such assurance seems unreal if you do not believe in His mercy, that He has forgiven you, accepted you and loves you – perfectly and for all eternity.

It is ludicrous to suggest that faith in God's mercy, grace and love will lead to disobedient, careless living. Quite the opposite, for Jesus continued by saying:

> If you obey my commands, you will remain in my love, just as I have obeyed my Father's commands and remain in his love. (John 15:10)

This is not to suggest that your obedience, your 'good works' cause you to be saved. Jesus obeyed His Father because He knew He was already totally loved and accepted by Him; His Father was well pleased with Him. Obedience enabled Him to abide or dwell in that love.

The same is true for you. If you disobey the Lord, He does not stop loving you – His love for you is eternal! But disobedience hinders your relationship with Him: you will not enjoy His love if you persist in offending that love. As soon as you acknowledge your sin and return to obedience,

God lovingly restores you. Once again you are at peace with Him and with yourself. And once again you flow together with Him in a deep bond of love. **You obey His words, not to cause God to love and accept you, but because He has already loved and accepted you in Jesus**.

Jesus knew the Father's love and so wanted to express that love to others in His teaching, His relationships, His miracles and through the healings and deliverances He performed. And, supremely, on the cross.

If you know Jesus's love, you want to express that love to others. You want them to know this great and wonderful love for themselves!

> A new command I give you: love one another. As I have loved you, so you must love one another. By this all men will know that you are my disciples, if you love one another. (John 13:34–35)

And yet many let their fear to witness to others quench this love that the Holy Spirit has placed in them. They want to speak of His love yet are afraid to do so.

At Kingdom Faith, people were becoming more outward-looking and concerned for the lost. There was much prayer for a move of God among unsaved people, that they would be drawn into God's Kingdom and become effective members of the church. We needed God to touch our hearts in such a way that we became motivated and confident in evangelistic outreach. His love within us would be so strong that it would overcome our natural fears. We wanted to bear much fruit and see the rich harvest God had been promising us.

However, we did not have any romantic ideas of revival, that suddenly God would sweep multitudes into the Kingdom while we stood idly by and watched. No, the Lord would need harvesters. He tells us to pray for them. This we did, conscious of the fact that God wanted us to be the answer to our own prayer. He wanted to make us effective reapers.

He wants children whose hearts are filled with His love,

who delight to do His will, who will be prepared to love others regardless of the cost, laying down their lives for others. He wants joyful obedience. We could not change our own hearts, but needed to allow Him to work the necessary changes in us. And He was leading us towards the point of anointing when He would do this!

We had to fulfil the great commission and go and make disciples. It was important, though, that those drawn into the church should be able to take their place in a body of believers who truly loved one another, and were learning what it meant to lay down their lives for their friends. To do this we each had to be totally secure in God's love for us!

13

The Victory of God's Love for You

God loved you long before you were aware of His love:

> But God demonstrates his own love for us in this: while we were still sinners, Christ died for us. (Rom. 5:8)

Jesus died for you, and took you to the cross to die with Him, **because He loves you**. And He has chosen to reveal the truth of the gospel to you **because He loves you**. He has come to live in you by His Holy Spirit **because He loves you**. He has placed His own love in you **because He loves you**.

All this is truth for you to accept. To live by faith is to make the right decisions, to believe the truth rather than what you see or feel. His love is a fact that can never change – He loves you because He is love. **He loves you because He loves you**. He needs no other reason. And His love for you has nothing to do with what you have or have not done. It is enough that you are His child by the new birth He has given you. And He continues His loving care of you, for never are you out of His presence:

> And we know that in all things God works for the good of those who love him, who have been called according to his purpose. (Rom. 8:28)

This is something we 'know', says Paul. It is not a matter of discussion, debate or contention. It is truth for all who respond to His love by loving Him. In all things God is working for your good, bringing you to the fulfilment of the purpose for which He has called you. **Nothing can separate you from His love**, no matter how difficult the circumstances:

> Who shall separate us from the love of Christ? Shall trouble or hardship or persecution or famine or nakedness or danger or sword? . . . No, in all these things we are more than conquerors through him who loved us. (Rom. 8:35,37)

You are to live in victory because you are 'more than a conqueror'. A conqueror is one who fights and establishes the victory by his efforts. One who is more than a conqueror does not fight for the victory; it has already been won. He receives that victory from the only one who can give it, from the one who loves him, from Jesus.

> Thanks be to God! He gives us the victory through our Lord Jesus Christ. (1 Cor. 15:57)

He gives you the victory. It does not matter what the situation, you will overcome if Christ is your victory. You will know the truth:

> Neither height nor depth, nor anything else in all creation, will be able to separate us from the love of God that is in Christ Jesus our Lord. (Rom. 8:39)

How can the love that God has for you enable you to be victorious? If you try to walk in your own strength, rather than His, you have returned to a religion of works, as if to say, 'I can only be holy by my own efforts. I can only overcome sin and difficulty and grasp opportunities by my own strength. I can only be victorious through my works.'

Even though you may ask God to help you, it is still

you that is trying to be victorious instead of receiving the gift of victory from God. Salvation is His gift; and so is victory! It is part of the total saving work that God has already accomplished for us in Jesus! It is a victory given us in love.

It would be folly to deny such a perfect gift and instead substitute our own effort. Every one of us has tried to be victorious in countless ways, and failed countless times! It cannot be done. We suppress many of our inadequacies instead of truly knowing victory in those areas of our lives. We trust to ourselves, instead of trusting in God's grace.

Remember, anything you earn or deserve cannot be grace. We cannot earn or deserve victory through our own righteous efforts. We have all tried to do so, and failed. We can only receive God's grace, or His love, or His victory as gifts from Him.

Why do we still struggle to do things in our own strength? Because we do not trust Jesus fully. **We do not believe that if we stop struggling He will undertake for us**; and so we continue to struggle! We imagine that if we do not fight for ourselves, He will not fight for us! This is false thinking.

Often God cannot do for us what He wants to do because we are still struggling to do it ourselves! While we are still trying to do things in our own strength, we clearly do not reckon ourselves 'dead'; neither are we trusting Him to work through us and for us.

Imagine a small boy who has a broken toy. He struggles unsuccessfully to mend it himself. His father offers to help, but the boy stubbornly refuses to accept any assistance. 'No,' he protests, 'I will do it myself.' His efforts end in futility. Finally in frustration he has to bury his pride and go to his father: 'Please, Dad, will you do it?' The father takes the toy and with his greater strength and ability mends it in a few moments!

How often are Christians like that boy. They struggle out of frustration and failure, often not praying about a situation, and even more frequently not realising that they only have to stop and surrender to the greater strength and ability of Jesus, and He will enable them to overcome! Behind our determination to struggle on in our own strength lie serious attitudes of unbelief and pride!

We try to be patient instead of realising that He is our patience.
We try to be strong instead of acknowledging that He is our strength.
We try to be holy instead of believing that He is our holiness.
We want to be victorious, failing to trust that He alone is our victory.
We try to change ourselves instead of acknowledging that Jesus is our life.

If you live by faith in God's Word and all that He has accomplished for you in His love, then you have to acknowledge that: **Jesus is your victory. In Him you have perfect victory! God has placed you in Him, so that His life becomes your life, His love the love within you, His victory your only way of truly overcoming**.

God has done more than change your life; He has exchanged your life with His life. When you were born again He did not look at the filthy rags of your self-righteousness and send them to the cleaners. He took them off and clothed you with Christ, so that you would no longer try to please Him with your own efforts, but lovingly accept that He is your all in all.

If God *gives* you the victory through Jesus, this has nothing to do with your efforts. A gift is a gift. Every time you trust Him, He works through you despite your weakness and failure. The flesh will always be weak, but the Spirit of God within you is strong. The Lord is bringing you to the point where instead of trusting in the weakness of your self-life, you trust in the power of God's Spirit within you!

When a Christian struggles in some area, often feeling a

failure, he tends to look at himself and his faults. He may go to his pastor or some counsellor for help. Often, the kind of advice he is given confirms his own estimate of the situation, that the fault lies in him. And so together they search for the fault, the reason for his failure. They delve into his past seeking the reason for his weakness. He is advised to persevere, is encouraged by being told that everybody fails – but God still loves him!

He needs to be pointed to the truth: **that it is impossible for him to gain the victory in any other way than by faith in what Jesus has already done for him.** It does not matter how weak that self-life is. God is so mighty, He can still work through him.

'Without faith it is impossible to please God.' No matter what the situation, the answer will only come through faith. Faith enables you to trust in the victory God has given you in Christ, not in your own strength or weakness or failure. Because He is merciful He forgives your sin, so that the power of His Spirit can be expressed through you. Do not concentrate on yourself, for the secret is: Christ in you, the hope of glory!

God said to Paul: 'My grace is sufficient for you, for my power is made perfect in weakness' (2 Cor. 12:9). This enabled him to 'delight in weaknesses, in insults, in hardships, in persecutions, in difficulties. For when I am weak, then I am strong' (2 Cor. 12:10).

The gospel is the same for you as for Paul; the truth is the same and the victory is the same! Instead of resenting the difficulties that arise you can rejoice in the Lord always, knowing that He *always* leads you in His triumphant procession, such is the grace that He wants to work in your life! The sad thing is that in recognising your weakness, you can struggle to be stronger in yourself, instead of realising your strength is in Him.

When the Lord confronted us with these truths, it was as if He was challenging us by asking: 'How far are you prepared to trust me?' Later I came to see that this was preparing us for what lay ahead, when we would have to learn to flow with the anointing that He gave us. We had to learn how to release that anointing so that His life and strength were expressed through us, instead of our own weakness.

We also had to appreciate that our weakness and failure did not disqualify us for revival! This would not come as a reward for our saintliness, but as a gift of God's grace. We could not work for it, only allow the Lord to lead us forward in His purposes.

Paul could testify that when he was weak, then he was strong, for he realised that he would always be weak in himself, and dare not trust in himself. He would inevitably fail if he was to do so. His trust had to be in Jesus and in the power of the Holy Spirit. In any and every situation God would undertake for him.

And he had to trust the Lord in the most trying of circumstances, 'beaten, and yet not killed; sorrowful, yet always rejoicing; poor, yet making many rich; having nothing, and yet possessing everything'(2 Cor. 6:9–10). Because of his faith, Paul could always be positive, knowing that Jesus would lead him through victoriously; even through beatings, stoning, shipwreck, constant danger, hunger and cold (see 2 Cor. 11:23–29). In many of these situations there was no point in trusting in himself; his confidence had to be in God and in God alone.

This is real faith expressed in practical everyday situations. Paul could not play spiritual games pretending he had victory when he had none. He had to learn how to trust God and let Him give him the victory in every situation. He believed that whatever God allowed him to go through would somehow benefit the cause of His Kingdom. He was not resentful about the cost he had to face; he kept rejoicing always. He knew that 'death' might be at work in him, but 'life' would be at work in others as a result.

Similarly, the Lord showed us that we could face our weakness and realise that He would ensure that we would always remain weak in ourselves, so that we would find our confidence in Him, that He would be our victory in every situation.

God has chosen the weak to confound the strong. He urges the weak to say they are strong, not in themselves but in Him!

Most of us realised we had a life of mixture. Sometimes we trusted Jesus and saw a measure of victory in our lives; at other times we failed to trust Him and felt overcome by the situation. When we looked at areas of failure we felt totally incapable of coming through to victory. This was particularly true of areas of sin that had afflicted us for so long that we could not conceive how we could ever be set free from them, even though we had experienced God's power in other areas of our lives.

We had to see that Christ Himself is our victory in *every* area of our lives.

When you appreciate that it is impossible for *you* to please God, you will allow Jesus to be your Victor. So long as you think *you* can please Him, then you have no incentive to trust Him. 'It is no longer I, but Christ,' says Paul, and he therefore comes to the inevitable conclusion that 'the life I live in the body, I live by faith in the Son of God, who loved me and gave himself for me' (Gal. 2:20).

Suppose you possess an old, well-used, but dilapidated car. You can have it repaired, resprayed, the rust holes filled in, the worn parts replaced. You would end with one repair bill after another. Alternatively, you can trade the old car in for a brand-new model!

Jesus did not come to keep repairing your life. He has replaced your life with His life. It would be expensive to trade an old, dilapidated car for a new one. It has cost you nothing to have your old life replaced! **This new life He has given you is a Person, Christ in you! You are victorious only because Christ lives in you.**

No amount of self-effort will enable you to change yourself. And every such effort is a denial of the faith you are to have in what Jesus has done for you. God does not give you victory in some areas of your personal life, or in difficult situations, as a reward for your efforts, but as a gift of His grace and love! That victory is free! But as with any gift it has to be received.

Remember, Jesus makes clear that in your flesh, in your self-life, there is nothing good. So you will never succeed in pleasing Him with that self-life. **You can only please Him by allowing His life in you to be expressed through you. That life is Christ Himself, the Victorious One!**

You will never overcome pride, lust, jealousy or any form of temptation by your own efforts. The only way to stand firm against temptation is through Jesus, not through yourself. **He is your Rock, your Shield, your Defence, your Fortress, your Victory.**

All that striving to improve yourself has come to nothing. And God has had to break you of the pride that caused you to think that you could overcome in your own strength. Many who lament their weakness and failure imagine they are humble because they have such a low opinion of themselves and their abilities. In reality they are often guilty of the pride that trusts in self instead of in Jesus.

Those with a strong self-life and great natural ability can please themselves through their own efforts. They will only please God by dying to self and letting His life be expressed in them. No matter how great their natural abilities, these are as nothing compared with the supernatural life and ability that is theirs in Christ.

In His humanity, Jesus was more capable than any other man who has ever lived. And yet He never trusted in Himself. He walked with perfect faith in the Father, total dependence on Him and complete submission to His will. He made it clear that He had not come to do His own will, but the will of Him who sent Him (John 6:38), that He could do nothing of Himself. If that was true for the Son of God, then it is certainly also true that we can do nothing worthwhile of ourselves!

Satan's desire when he tempted Jesus in the wilderness

was to persuade Him to do something on His own initiative, independently from His Father. This Jesus steadfastly refused to do:

> Man does not live by bread alone, but on every word that comes from the mouth of God. (Matt. 4:4)

And so it must be for us. We are not to act according to the suggestions of the world, the flesh or the devil. We are alive in Christ to please Him and to glorify the Father, and we will only succeed in doing that by obeying the voice of the Holy Spirit. He can work through us despite our weakness. He can enable us to live victoriously beyond anything we could imagine. And He will enable us to be a blessing to others, often working supernaturally through us, despite our own personal inadequacies.

God does not wait until you attain a certain level of holiness before Jesus becomes your victory. He is your victory now!

When you trust to yourself, you will fail – and God allows you to do so. You can confess the sins of your failure, and He will be merciful and will forgive you. But inevitably you will return to the same sins. Forgiveness is not the same as having the victory over sin. It is wonderful to be forgiven; it is even more wonderful to have the victory over sin. Lack of such victory deprives the believer of confidence.

Many believers have such a history of failure they cannot see how they could ever have such victory. Just as God *gave* you salvation as a free gift of His grace and love, so He *gives* you victory over sin. While you fight in your own strength, though, you cannot live in the good of His victory! You do not gain victory by degrees, but as a gift! Sin shall not have dominion over you. It shall not be your master, because you are no longer under law but under grace. 'The law of the Spirit of life set me free from the law of sin and death' (Rom. 8:2).

Law is man trying to please God. Grace is God giving to

man. The old law of trying to please God with self has now been replaced by a new law: God's own Spirit at work within you, so that His life of victory, not your life of failure, can find expression in your daily circumstances.

When you try to work for God, sin rules over you. **When you let God work for you, you rule over sin!** What a difference!

If these things are true why do so many Christians still live in such fear and failure? The answer can only be because they are either ignorant of the truth, or do not believe it!

There is nothing further that God has to do to enable you to be victorious. He has already given you that victory through Jesus. You need to believe this. Many are reluctant to do so because they keep looking at themselves and their failure, instead of at Him and His provision! Their vision of His grace and love is so limited!

Jesus did more on the cross than to die for your forgiveness. He died to break the power of sin in your life! That happens only when you accept Jesus as your victory. You 'receive God's abundant provision of grace and of the gift of righteousness' and so are able to 'reign in life through the one man, Jesus Christ' (Rom. 5:17).

You will never reign in life through your own efforts. To reign through Jesus is not to persist in the same syndromes of sin, fear and failure that have persisted for years.

Many Christians have accepted a lifetime of failure and defeat for themselves and so hate to hear talk of triumph and victory. They have tried so hard and failed so often, they are convinced these things are beyond them. They have never accepted Jesus as their victory. So they stumble on in their own strength and failure!

You did not need to beg for salvation, or to fast for a prolonged period of time to acquire it. You turned to God in repentance and faith and received your salvation as His gift to you. Even so with all God's gifts. A gift is not acquired by effort, prolonged prayer and fasting. No, **God's gifts are acquired through faith** and are given in a moment of time.

No amount of self-effort can earn salvation. No amount of self-effort can acquire victory.

It is as if two people live within, self and Christ, and the two are often at odds! Instead of victory there seems to be much conflict.

Victory over sin is not suppression of that sin. It is not putting on a mask to hide its presence. It is the miracle of God's grace and love for you; His life, instead of yours, is manifested. If you are still fighting for the victory, you clearly have not received it as a gift of God's grace!

This is the point at which an important decision has to be made. Someone has to go! Obviously I do not want Christ to leave me, so 'I' has to go. And that is as it should be, for it was for this reason that 'I' was crucified with Christ. I have to leave the ground clear for Christ in me to take control.

However, there may be several occasions on which you have come to that conclusion and even prayed that there may be less of you and more of Jesus in your life. Therein lies your mistake, for there is not to be less of you, but *no* you. That 'I' has been crucified with Christ. God's judgement on your self-life is that it is totally useless and worthy only of death. He has already judged that life on the cross. Now all you have to do is first to recognise that Jesus's judgement was correct and then agree that He has dealt with that old self on the cross.

This is not a question of realising you ought to die or should try to put yourself to death. **You have died and your life is already hidden with Christ in God.**

If Jesus has taken that life to the cross, then why are you so weak, still defeated and sometimes overcome by sin? Why are you not more like Jesus and walking in His victory? You may even have tried reckoning yourself dead to sin and that doesn't seem to work either!

If you truly accepted that God's judgement on your self-life was right, you would not struggle for the survival of that self-life, neither would you try to please God by your own efforts. Still you trust in yourself – at least to some degree. And that is sufficient to deprive you of the victory God wants for you.

We are not talking of some advanced spirituality for particularly saintly people, but of God's intention for every believer. His assessment of every one of us is that in our self-life we are worthless and useless, without hope. Only in Christ do we find acceptance and our true worth.

Jesus did not come to improve us, but to crucify us and make us new. That new life is Christ in you. Self has to step aside in order for you to be able to live that new life. As long as you try to improve yourself you have not accepted God's assessment of that self-life. As long as you try to please Him with your own efforts you contradict Him by suggesting there is some value in that self-life, and that you can use it to do something that would please Him.

We readily appreciate that we could not improve ourselves before we were saved. Why should we think we are any more capable of improving ourselves after we have been saved? And yet we often resolve to do better; we make promises, only to discover that we lose our resolve and break them! We think we have come to the point of despairing of self, and yet continue to keep that self-life very much alive! So what can I do to resolve this dilemma?

I have to come to the point where I agree with God about myself: I am completely and utterly useless. You may have felt like that at times but then have done everything you could to pull yourself together, instead of allowing Jesus to be your victory! You have readily identified with Paul's dilemma:

> I do not understand what I do. For what I want to do I do not do, but what I hate I do. (Rom. 7:15)

He continues by giving his reason for giving way to sin:

> As it is, it is no longer I myself who do it, but it is sin living in me. I know that nothing good lives in me, that is, in my sinful nature. (v. 17–18)

He recognises that nothing good lives in his flesh or self-life. But it is not his new self that sins; this is the result of 'sin living in me'.

> Now if I do what I do not want to do, it is no longer I who do it, but it is sin living in me that does it. (v. 20)

This sin wages war with his new nature that wants to do what is right. What is the solution to his dilemma? He cries out in anguish: 'What a wretched man I am! Who will rescue me from this body of death?' And then he gives the answer:

> Thanks be to God – through Jesus Christ our Lord! (v. 25)

Only Jesus can be the answer. **The believer can only overcome sin by accepting the victory of Jesus**. And so in the very next verse Paul affirms:

> Therefore, there is now no condemnation for those who are in Christ Jesus, because through Christ Jesus the law of the Spirit of life set me free from the law of sin and death. (Rom. 8:1–2)

It is of the greatest importance to accept that Jesus has already done for you everything necessary to give you the victory. He has *already* set you free from the law of sin and death. Paul continues:

> For what the law was powerless to do in that it was weakened by the sinful nature, God did by sending his own Son in the likeness of sinful man to be a sin offering. (Rom. 8:3)

God did for you what you could not do for yourself. Now 'the righteous requirements of the law can be fully met in you', not because you are trying to obey God in your own strength, but **because you are trusting Him to be your life**.

So first you accept God's judgement on your self-life, that it is worthy only of crucifixion. Then you can be thankful that in Christ that crucifixion has already taken place. Sin need no longer be your master because Jesus has delivered you from the power of sin. You sin only when you trust in that self-life, or try to please Him with that self-life. All that remains now is to acknowledge that God has given you the victory.

You may say: 'Well, what can I do to get that victory?' The answer to that is simple: 'Nothing!' Herein lies the whole issue. So long as 'I' think that 'I' am able to achieve this victory 'I' am still trusting in 'I' – not Him; I am not living out the truth that 'I no longer live'!

I can do nothing, only accept what He has done for me. He has already given me victory in Christ Jesus.

And so you come to the conclusion: 'Lord, there is absolutely nothing I can do to please you. I am so useless in myself that I give up trying to please you.' This at first sounds radical, even wrong. And yet I have found that while I strive to accomplish something, I fail. As soon as I acknowledge I can do nothing, stop trying and leave the ground clear for Jesus to work, there is victory. Jesus said:

> If anyone would come after me, he must deny himself and take up his cross and follow me. For whoever wants to save his life will lose it, but whoever loses his life for me will find it. (Matt. 16:24–25)

You live in Christ because God has placed you in Him. By denying yourself you **allow His life to be your life. Then His love, His joy and peace, His righteousness and holiness, His power, His victory and His glory will be revealed in you**.

None of this is beyond you. It is for this that God called and chose you, and placed you in Christ. If you have a low opinion of yourself you have an advantage, for it should be easier to stop trusting in yourself, to stop defending yourself or seek to find some worth in your self-life. **You do not have to accomplish anything to make Jesus's life your life. He already is! You only have to believe that He is**! The life of His Spirit will then be manifested through your life in the way God intends.

You do not have to overcome gradually by your own efforts if you believe Christ has already overcome and is your victory. Watchman Nee puts this point very clearly:

> How do we receive this gift? By doing nothing: Let us simply accept it. As we believe God's Word, we receive this gift. This is the gospel. We receive by faith, and the Holy Spirit takes our faith to be the starting point for God's miracle to be done in us. People who have not experienced the mighty power of God may not take this seriously. But to the experienced, it is a precious reality. As we believe that all which is in the Lord is ours, the Holy Spirit will cause it to be truly ours. What a gospel this is! Whatever belongs to Christ becomes ours through faith! (*The Life that Wins*, p.59)

What are you to do if you surrender all to the Lord, tell Him that you have come to the end of yourself and that you give up trying to please Him with your own efforts – and nothing happens? You may sense or feel nothing, nor see any immediate change. Are you still to believe you have the victory? Yes!

Jesus taught us: 'Whatever you ask in prayer, believe that you have received it, and it will be yours' (Mark 11:24). **When you believe you have the victory, you will see results**. If you look for results to determine whether you have the victory or not, then clearly you are not in a position of faith. **Results follow faith; they do not precede faith**.

You need to proclaim that you have the overcoming victorious life, even before you see the evidence of it. If you cannot speak victory you do not truly believe you have victory in Christ. From the overflow of what you believe in your heart, your mouth will speak! It is better to speak of your victory in Christ than of your own inadequacy and failure! This is not playing games with formulas of words.

Yield your self-life to Him in a decisive way, believe that you have His life and victory as your life, and you will begin to experience radical change. You will be free and will have a closer fellowship and walk with Jesus than you ever imagined possible!

The enemy will try to persuade you that nothing has changed because when you make the decision you do not have any great sensation or experience. He will try to encourage you to look for results before you believe. He will suggest that you cannot be victorious if you do not feel victorious! He will accuse you when you sin, suggesting you could not have Jesus as your victory or you would not have sinned.

In other words, the enemy wants you to concentrate on your self-life. He wants that to be the controlling factor in your life, for then he knows you will suffer defeat after defeat.

What God has done for you in Christ is true and eternal. It never changes with time, circumstances or feelings. When you stop fighting, God fights for you. He has already overcome the enemy on the cross. So His victory becomes your victory, not only in overcoming personal issues, but also in overcoming the devil. Believe Jesus to be your Victor; the enemy has no answer to such faith! He will do whatever he can to persuade you to hold on to self and not come to a place of full submission and surrender to Jesus. Instead of giving up on yourself, he wants you to believe that there is some value to your self-life. He will even suggest that this must be so because God created you in His image. Because you are not totally depraved, there must be some good in you. Sadly, he often succeeds in such appeals; he is the deceiver of the brethren.

Once you have exchanged Christ's life for yours, His victory for your failure, the enemy has no answer. Of course he does not give up; he tries to persuade you to return to the life of self. Even when you do sin, you have God's mercy; there is no condemnation for you because you are in Christ. Instead of dwelling on your failure, return immediately to the victory ground on which you stand in Him.

What Jesus did for you, He accomplished without your help – and He will **give** you the victory without your help! Such is God's amazing love for you. Where you have constantly failed, He succeeds on your behalf! You will be amazed at the difference when instead of worrying about your weakness, you simply use your failure as a springboard to trust more fully in God's mercy, grace and love.

14

Expressing the Father's Love

To live in revival is to live as a son of God, with all the responsibilities and privileges this involves. Jesus died and rose again that He may lead many sons to glory! And we who have put our faith in Him and are born again of God's Spirit are those sons.

> For you did not receive a spirit that makes you a slave again to fear, but you received the Spirit of sonship. And by him we cry, 'Abba, Father.' The Spirit himself testifies with our spirit that we are God's children. Now if we are children, then we are heirs – heirs of God and co-heirs with Christ, if indeed we share in his sufferings in order that we may also share in his glory. (Rom. 8:15–17)

The fact that you have received the gift of God's Holy Spirit is the evidence that He has accepted you and made you His child. He is your Father and His Spirit is the guarantee of your eternal inheritance. Not only is He your Father now; He always will be your Father!

Jesus lived and died for you so that you can know and relate to Him as your Father. You live in Christ so that you can be a co-heir with Him of all the Father has to give.

> Because you are sons, God sent the Spirit of his Son into our hearts, the Spirit who calls out, 'Abba, Father.' So you are no longer a slave, but a son; and since you are a son, God has made you also an heir. (Gal. 4:6–7)

Paul emphasises God's activity; He sent the Spirit of Jesus into your heart so that you know and relate to Him as your Father.

He has made you an heir with Christ of all that He has to give. **God has chosen you to inherit from Him all that Jesus inherits.** By faith you have already begun to enter into that inheritance. He is your righteousness. He is your holiness. He is your life. He is your victory. He is your healer, your provider, and so on.

Because you are fully accepted in Him, you are fully loved by the Father. **Because you are in His Beloved Son, He treats you as He treats Jesus. He wants to lavish on you all the riches of His grace and love.** It is only reluctance to believe in this amazing love that causes God to be limited in your life, and the flow of His blessings to be stunted. He is always more ready to give than you are to receive. Nobody can make himself an heir; God chose you for this wonderful privilege.

In his first letter, the apostle John says: 'Our fellowship is with the Father and with his Son, Jesus Christ' (1:3). Because you are in Christ you have fellowship with God as your Father. The word 'fellowship' means 'the sharing of life'. Because you share in the life of the Son, you share in the life of the Father. 'Whoever acknowledges the Son has the Father also' (1 John 2:23). And the Holy Spirit lives in you! So the whole Trinity of God is involved intimately in your life.

In Him there is no darkness. And so we are called to share fellowship with light. As we do this we are made one with others who walk in the light and share fellowship with the Father, Son and Holy Spirit.

John's first letter is an epistle about love, the loving relationships that we are to have with God and with one another. The way in which we relate to God affects deeply the way we relate to other people. If we know God in His mercy, we will be merciful to others. If we know God's grace we will abound in graciousness ourselves. If we know this full acceptance we will be far more accepting of others – and so on. The more we know His love, the more loving we will be towards others.

> How great is the love the Father has lavished on us, that we should be called children of God! And that is what we are! (1 John 3:1)

How great is the love behind the fact that He gave Christ to be our life, our righteousness, holiness, Lord, Saviour, Healer and Provider. Love requires a response of love. This has to be a voluntary response on our part. God could not force us to love Him. Even the heavenly creatures had to be free to love; the Lord could not make them so that they had to love Him automatically. Satan began as an angel leading the worship in heaven. When he abused his position by wanting to become the object of worship himself, he was thrown out of heaven.

So God does not force us to love. He shows more and more of His love for us, and desires us to respond in love. **He fills us with the Spirit of love, giving us the capacity to love Him and others, but without forcing us to express that love.**

Jesus makes it clear that those who love God will obey what He commands. Such obedience is the consequence of genuine love for Him. When we fail in our love, He does not throw us out of His Kingdom; we have Someone interceding there on our behalf! Jesus intercedes with His own blood which is able to cleanse us from all sin. Once again we see the provision of God's mercy towards us.

To know God is to love Him. We cannot possibly know Him as He really is without loving Him. And the better we know Him, the greater our love will be!

To obey God's Word is to believe what He says and to put it into action. **We believe what He says; and then we live in this revelation of the truth.** It would be both unloving and disbelieving to do otherwise.

> But if anyone obeys his word, God's love is truly made complete in him. This is how we know we are in him. (1 John 2:5)

We have seen that loving God is not doing our own thing *for* God. It is letting Him express His life in and through us because we trust Him and walk in fellowship with Him.

> Whoever claims to live in him must walk as Jesus did. (1 John 2:6)

This is not an option, it is a 'must'. However, this can only be done through our free response of love. There is little point in claiming these wonderful truths about our life in Christ, if we do not live in the good of them.

Because we live in Jesus we are to walk in the truth, in the revelation of God's Word. He has given us the Spirit of Truth to guide us into all the truth. We are to walk in obedience to that truth because we walk in love for God. We are to walk in the light as the children of light. That love and obedience is shown in the way in which we love other people.

> Whoever loves his brother lives in the light, and there is nothing in him to make him stumble. (1 John 2:10)

By contrast, those who fail to love their brothers are still in darkness, the truth is not in them. John uses strong language to state these truths bluntly and unequivocally. He also says that we cannot love the world (by which he means worldliness) if we love the Father.

> For everything in the world – the cravings of sinful man, the lust of his eyes and the boasting of what he has and does – comes not from the Father but from the world. (1 John 2:16)

God has anointed you so that you may know the truth and have the power to obey what He says: 'You have an anointing from the Holy One, and all of you know the truth' (2:20). The Holy Spirit keeps reminding you of the truth of what Jesus has done for you.

> See that what you have heard from the beginning remains in you. If it does, you also will remain in the Son and in the Father. (1 John 2:24)

The anointing of the Holy Spirit 'teaches you about all things' pertaining to your life in Christ. Even if some churches do not teach this truth, the Holy Spirit always does! So where the truth is not taught you know there is a distinct absence of the Holy Spirit in the pulpit!

It is folly to sit under any teaching other than the truth, for only the truth of who God is and what He has done for you will build your faith. Man's wisdom and ideas, no matter how well intentioned or pleasantly expressed, will never have that effect. Faith comes from hearing God's Word, the words of the Bible.

The Holy Spirit will urge you to continue to live in Him, in His love, with Jesus as your Victor – always leading you in His triumphant procession.

> And now, dear children, continue in him, so that when he appears we may be confident and unashamed before him at his coming. (1 John 2:28)

To continue in Him is to live as a child of God, dependent on Him. And the Father has lavished His love upon you to enable you to do this. Those who live in Him will not persist in sin; they will trust to the life of Christ's Spirit within to enable them to overcome.

John affirms: 'He who does what is right is righteous' (1 John 3:7). No super-spirituality here! No cheap grace! He urges his readers to live according to their position in Christ and makes it clear that as they do so, this will have practical implications: they will not persist in sin, but will manifest the righteousness of Jesus. They will look to Him to give them the victory when they are under attack.

This does not imply that we will automatically, suddenly, walk in perfection. There always seems to be an area of our lives where we find it impossible to overcome in our own strength, no matter how hard we try.

Paul had mighty revelations and experiences of God. Yet he was given 'a thorn in my flesh, a messenger of Satan, to torment me' (2 Cor. 12:7). We do not need to conjecture what the thorn represented; that is unimportant to our present discussion. We need to see first why God allowed Paul to have this thorn: 'To keep me from becoming conceited' (v. 7). This was His way of preventing Paul from becoming proud because of the ways in which he experienced God working in his life.

Second, we need to see the Lord's response when Paul pleaded three times for this 'thorn' to be removed.

> My grace is sufficient for you, for my power is made perfect in weakness. (2 Cor. 12:9)

Paul had to keep trusting in God's grace. **For the Christian life is grace, followed by grace, followed by grace, followed by grace, followed by grace.** It is *not* grace followed by your own works and striving.

God's supply of grace for you is always sufficient for the situation. As Paul trusted to the Lord in his difficulties, God's enabling would cause him to triumph. In his weakness he would cast himself on the Lord in faith, and God's power would be expressed in his life.

Notice that Paul does not say that God gives him the power to enable him to overcome. No, it is *Christ's* power resting on him! So Paul will have no cause to boast. The same principle is true for each one of us.

God never loses sight of you, or of the situation you are in. ***His* grace is available and will prove sufficient. *His***

power will be manifest in your weakness as you put your trust in Him.

God does not ask you to love Him with all your heart, mind, soul and strength, without giving you His resources of love to do so. He does not ask you to love others as He has loved you, without giving you His own quality of love.

> This is how we know what love is: Jesus Christ laid down his life for us. And we ought to lay down our lives for our brothers. (1 John 3:16)

This sounds fine, but what does it mean? Jesus lived for others, not Himself. He came to fulfil the Father's will, not His own. He lived for His Father, not Himself. He wanted to please the Father, not Himself. This is love for God. And He devoted Himself whole-heartedly to live in such a way.

He lived for others by the selfless way in which He poured Himself out in ministry. However, He never allowed anything to weaken His relationship with, and dependence on, the Father. If He was so busy ministering to the needs of others, He would draw aside to be alone with His Father, even if this involved praying all night!

Jesus knew that the strength of His unity with the Father was essential for His love of the people. So when He had to face the supreme act of love on the cross, He drew aside to pray in the Garden, submitting afresh to His Father's will.

We can love others because Jesus has laid down His life for us. His Spirit of love lives in us. I cannot love with His love in the way He expects by depending on my own weak resources of love. I need to let His love be expressed through me. How? **By submitting myself, all that I am and have, to Jesus; just as He submitted Himself to the will of His Father.** This will have very practical implications:

> If anyone has material possessions and sees his brother in need but has no pity on him, how can the love of God be in him? (1 John 3:17)

As long as the believer is holding on to what he has for himself, he is still holding on to 'self'. This can prevent Jesus from being his Victor in practical situations. All of us reap what we sow. If we sow to please ourselves, that is all we will accomplish; but if we sow to please God, he will give His full measure back to us. Jesus said:

> Then the King will say to those on his right, 'Come, you who are blessed by my Father; take your inheritance, the kingdom prepared for you since the creation of the world. For I was hungry and you gave me something to eat, I was thirsty and you gave me something to drink, I was a stranger and you invited me in, I needed clothes and you clothed me, I was sick and you looked after me, I was in prison and you came to visit me.' (Matt. 25:34–36)

Those who consider themselves 'super-spiritual', like the Pharisees, avoid the needs placed in front of them. No wonder John says:

> Dear children, let us not love with words or tongue but with actions and in truth. (1 John 3:18)

The Spirit within us urges us to love, give, serve, and He supplies the resources to do so.

When you trust Him, you find yourself able to love in situations where you do not feel loving, and where you would have no desire or natural ability to love. Yet when you yield to Him, His supernatural love is expressed through you. When you listen to the Spirit, He will work through you. The anointing you receive from Him will enable God to be received by others through you, even though in yourself you may feel weak, useless and inadequate.

Jesus had a serving, giving heart. He wants you to have such a heart!

To walk in obedience to Jesus, submitting to Him and trusting Him, enables you to have great confidence before God.

> Dear friends, if our hearts do not condemn us, we have confidence before God and receive from him anything we ask, because we obey his commands and do what pleases him. (1 John 3:21–22)

And what does please Him? That you do His will, *His* work. And what is His work? Jesus said: 'The work of God is this: to believe in the one he has sent' (John 6:29).

You will not please Him in your own strength or weakness, but only by trusting in Him! You will have confidence before God (as Jesus did), and will receive from Him anything you ask (as Jesus did)! Why? Because you obey His commands and do what pleases him. He then explains:

> And this is his command: to believe in the name of his Son, Jesus Christ, and to love one another as he commanded us. (I John 3:23)

This agrees exactly with what Jesus Himself said, as we would expect. There is a close relationship between faith and love. Paul says, likewise, that the only thing that counts is 'faith expressing itself through love' (Gal. 5:6).

There are those who try to set these in contradiction to each other. Either they say, 'I follow the way of love', implying that if you have love, faith is of little importance. Or they say: 'I'm a faith person', implying that faith is the only thing that matters and love is of much less significance.

Such distinctions do not accord with scripture. It is true: 'If I have a faith that can move mountains, but have not love, I am nothing' (1 Cor. 13:2). But it is also true that 'Everything that does not come from faith is sin' (Rom. 14:23). **It is not a question of faith or love, but faith in love! Both belong together.**

Paul gives us a wonderful description of the nature of God's love:

> Love is patient, love is kind. It does not envy, it does not boast, it is not proud. It is not rude, it is not self-seeking,

> it is not easily angered, it keeps no record of wrongs. Love does not delight in evil but rejoices with the truth. It always protects, always trusts, always hopes, always perseveres. Love never fails. (1 Cor. 13:4–8)

Is such a love beyond you? No, **it is within you!** These are the qualities of the Spirit of love God has placed in you.

There are many instances when you are not patient or kind; at times you may boast, be envious or proud. There may be occasions when you are rude, self-seeking and angry. You may find it difficult sometimes to forgive, harbouring grudges instead of keeping no record of wrongs, and so on. In other words there are many occasions when you know that you have failed to love with the kind of love described here.

You may try to love others better, trying harder to express the kind of love you ought to have and fail frequently. You can look at yourself, confess all the inadequacies of love, know God's forgiveness and still perform no better! Why not? Because this is a description of God's love; the qualities of His Spirit. He has placed that love in you. But every time *you* try to love, you will only express *your* love which is very pale, weak and ineffective by comparison. The only option is to acknowledge that *you* can never love like this, but *He* always does. So you will not try to love with your own strength but will trust Him to love with His love through you! This is the outworking of your faith.

Paul describes the fruit of the Spirit:

> But the fruit of the Spirit is love, joy, peace, patience, kindness, goodness, faithfulness, gentleness and self-control. Against such things there is no law. (Gal. 5:22–23)

Law, remember, is trying to please God with our own effort and works. You can never reproduce these qualities for yourself. They are the work of God's own Spirit living within you.

Because the Holy Spirit is God, He can only reproduce the qualities of God Himself. This means that He reproduces love in us because God is love. He produces joy in us because God is our joy, and He wants His joy to be in us and our joy to be full (John 15:11). Jesus stood among His disciples in His risen body and imparted peace to them as a gift because He is our peace.

God is love. He is joy. He is peace. He is patient with us. He is always kind, His mercies are new every morning. He is always good, and by His grace gives of His goodness to us in abundance. He is faithful, and His faithfulness endures for ever. He is gentle which is why Jesus described Himself as being 'gentle and humble of heart'. And only the Spirit of God can keep that self-life of ours under control so that His life can be expressed in us in the way that will bring glory to God.

You do not have to strive to make yourself like Him; indeed you are powerless to do this. The more you allow Him to be your life, living as one who has put on Christ, the more you will reflect Him in your character and actions, in the way you love others! This is His work, the work of His Spirit. You cannot accomplish these things for yourself or reproduce these qualities by any efforts of your own. This has to be the work of Christ working in you by His Spirit. The more you try in your strength, the more you will fail to reproduce Him in your life.

The greater your faith in God's love for you, the more His love can flow out of you to others.

> This is love: not that we loved God, but that he loved us and sent his Son as an atoning sacrifice for our sins. Dear friends, since God so loved us, we also ought to love one another. (1 John 4:10–11)

The more you know His love and trust in what He did for you on the cross, the more you will want to make His love known.

This will, of course, give you a great longing to see people saved. You will want to be a faithful witness to others of the gospel. Your desire to see people saved involves more than speaking of God's love; you will be prepared to demonstrate that love in practical ways, by serving and giving, regardless of the cost to yourself.

> God is love. Whoever lives in love lives in God, and God in him. In this way, love is made complete among us so that we will have confidence on the day of judgment, because in this world we are like him. (1 John. 4:16–17)

How can you ever be like Him in His love, unless you allow 'self' to step aside and let His love flow through you? You could never make yourself like God. The amazing truth is that **when you express the life of God's Spirit you really are like Him in the world! This is not some ideal that is beyond you. It is what God intends and what He has made possible by placing His Spirit within you**.

> There is no fear in love. But perfect love drives out fear, because fear has to do with punishment. The one who fears is not made perfect in love. (1 John 4:18)

When you realise that your responsibility is not to try to love with yourself, but to allow His love to flow through you, then you recognise that there is no need to fear. When you trust in yourself you fear failure, and rightly so. **When you trust God to release His love through you, then there is no fear, for He never fails. When you leave the way clear for Him to act, then you are assured that He will do so and the outcome will be successful**. For He knows and understands the situation better than you do. He knows exactly what is required in each situation and He will supply all that is needed by His grace.

Remember, you have perfect love within you because you have the Perfect One, who is love, within you. Fear has to do with punishment. But we have seen that God does not want to punish failure; He desires to teach us how to end the failure syndrome in our lives by not trusting in ourselves. We stop and *He* works! This is why He gives you anointing from the Holy Spirit. There really is no limit to what He can do through you.

> Everyone who loves the father loves his child as well. This is how we know that we love the children of God: by loving God and carrying out his commands. (1 John 5:1–2)

John makes clear that 'his commands are not burdensome' (1 John 5:3). They seem burdensome to us only when we do not want to obey, or think we are not able to obey because of inevitable failure. No command is burdensome if you believe that God will enable you, that He will do it in and through you. It will not be a burden if you believe you will succeed! And so John then says:

> And his commands are not burdensome, for everyone born of God overcomes the world. This is the victory that has overcome the world, even our faith. Who is it that overcomes the world? Only he who believes that Jesus is the Son of God. (1 John 5:3–5)

You have victory over the world when you live by faith. **Jesus will enable you to express His life in whatever way is right in any particular situation**. Instead of walking around with diffidence, almost apologising for your presence as a Christian, you can go in confidence knowing that you take the presence, the life and the love of Jesus into every situation. **Because you are clothed with Him, people will touch His life through you**. You may feel inadequate in yourself; nevertheless because you are in Him, He will be a shield about you. He will fight for you. He will be your defence when under attack. He will give you the words to speak and will show you what to do. The love within you will overcome your fears of reaching out to touch others.

As you read the Gospels, you see that Jesus won people by love. He was prepared to eat and socialise with sinners and outcasts. He did not go to them to evangelise them, to tell them that as sinners they were in danger of hell-fire. He went to love them. Of course He wanted to convey to them the good news of the Kingdom, to take them out of their life of sin and into a new life that He alone could give them. But He knew their greatest need was to know that God did not desire to condemn them, but in His love to save them and set them free.

Many Christians need to learn how to befriend the unsaved. It is not wasted time showing people that you love them and care about them. God has incarnated His love in you. If you love those who love you, what credit is there in that; even pagans do that. As a Christian you can reach out to those who could see no reason why you should want to love them or be so concerned about their needs.

The local church is to be an expression of the Body of Christ. That is a Body of love. Feeling love for people is not the same as expressing that love. If we look at our fears we are rendered powerless; but when we look to the Lord to be our life, His perfect love casts out the fear. The power of love (which is supernatural) is more powerful than our fears (which are only rational!).

> If we love one another, God lives in us and his love is made complete in us. (1 John 4:12)

The local congregation is to express a love and caring for one another that could be found nowhere else. To lay down your life for your friends is to prefer others, to live for them and not yourself. In reality people are often members of a particular church out of their personal preferences, rather than any conviction that this is where God has put them to love those who are part of that congregation; to live for the others instead of themselves. To love, serve and give to others!

Without hearts full of God's love, we are left with a list of things we ought to do, but with little or no motivation to do these things. This does not mean that we wait for the right feelings before doing anything. God's love is not an emotion; it is often expressed out of sheer obedience. **When you step out in obedience to what God says in His Word**, **you find the Holy Spirit gives you all the resources of God's love that you need**. Then others will not think that you only take interest in them out of a sense of duty, but out of genuine love and concern. You do not judge them, but want to express God's mercy and love to them. You want to introduce them to God's grace so that they can receive all the riches and resources He wants to pour into their lives. His commands are not burdensome when there is love in your heart!

God has placed His love in you. **Wherever you go, you are an ambassador of that love**. It may seem unfair, but nevertheless it is the case, that many non-Christians will evaluate God's love by what they see of His love in your life. You may want to protest that no matter how much you love, your expression of that love is far inferior to the true nature of God's love. That is, of course, true. But demonstrating His love and concern for people has to amount to more than telling people that God loves them or that you accept them. Such words may encourage them; but they still need to experience His love in practical ways.

Some consider themselves too 'spiritual' for this. What deception! For Jesus Himself came as the servant of all, who washed His disciples' feet and sat with the sinners to demonstrate His love and concern for them. And we are to love others as He has loved us!

With 'the mustard seed anointing' an amazing transformation came upon the church, for suddenly many were motivated to do what they knew they should, and in many cases wanted to do, but felt inadequate or afraid to accomplish. The anointing broke the yoke of this fear.

As a result, many began to witness in ways they had never done before. Some led others to faith in Christ for the first time. Not only did they have greater motivation; the anointing enabled them to become more effective. The power of God's love in them began to draw more and more people into the Kingdom, enabling the church to grow within a few weeks at four times that rate formerly experienced.

This was the first-fruits of revival.

15

Prayer

Prayer is the key to revival. From the beginning we taught people how to pray, aware that Kingdom Faith Church would need to be a praying church if we were to experience revival.

Yonggi Cho wrote a book entitled *Prayer, the Key to Revival*. And he should know the key to revival with a church of over 700,000. I asked Hector Gimenèz how important prayer was to the move of the Spirit his church was enjoying in Buenos Aires. His answer was simple: 'Prayer is everything.'

There is little point in knowing the centrality of prayer in God's purposes if we do not pray! However, the way we pray is of great importance. Many pray for revival and are frustrated because they never see or experience it.

The purpose of prayer is that we should meet with God and so strengthen our relationship with Him; that He should hear what is on our hearts and we should know what is on His.

The focus of our prayer at Kingdom Faith was to meet with God, for when you meet with Him you pray with great faith and expectation; your intercession becomes more effective, and you exercise greater authority over the enemy in spiritual warfare.

We are told to 'pray at all times in the Spirit'. This must mean that the Holy Spirit is to lead our prayer, and that He will also fill it with His presence and His power. Those of former generations who experienced revival spoke of the spirit of prayer being upon God's people. From the outset we knew this to be important for us. The spirit of prayer would come upon us only when we demonstrated our commitment to prayer by praying, by earnestly seeking the Lord with our hearts.

Five minutes of prayer can seem a long time to people without this anointing from the Holy Spirit. However, with the spirit of prayer, an hour can seem like five minutes. We struggle in our own strength; but we flow with God Himself when we do things in the power of His Spirit.

The fresh revelation of God's mercy, grace and love affected our lives in many practical ways, but especially our praying. We had a greater understanding of the One to whom we were praying. We had grown in our understanding of His mercy, that He was always ready to be merciful to us whenever we turned to Him. He had no desire to reject any of our prayers for personal healing, revival of the church and nation, or anything else.

He is the God of grace and wants His grace to abound to us, so that in all things at all times we would have everything we needed (2 Cor. 9:8). This verse is written over the platform in our worship centre at Roffey Place. It is a constant reminder to us of the nature of our God. Whether we think of Him as Father, Son or Holy Spirit, **He is gracious. He wants to give to us, and He delights to see the faith in our hearts that expects Him to pour one blessing after another into our lives.**

This commitment to prayer is expressed at Kingdom Faith in several different ways:

1 The Kingdom Faith Ministries' team, together with the students during term-time, meet from Monday to Friday at 8.00 a.m. for an hour of worship and prayer.
2 During preparation for revival weeks, and the revival conferences themselves, there is also corporate prayer from 1 to 2 p.m., instead of a lunch break!
3 On Sundays, there is half an hour of prayer before the morning service and this is open to all.

4 The main church prayer meeting precedes the evening service and lasts for an hour, or that is the intention. Frequently the Spirit is moving so powerfully in the prayer meeting that it runs on past the time when the service is due to begin. At least 90 per cent of the evening congregation attend the prayer meeting. As you can imagine, it makes all the difference to what God does in the service when virtually everybody has been praying for an hour beforehand! There have been occasions when the service never happened – the prayer meeting lasted for three hours!

   People are only going to come in hundreds to prayer meetings if the Lord is truly active and His presence obvious. If the Lord is there, the people will be there!

5 On week-day afternoons there is a Prayer School. Students are taught how to intercede and break through in spiritual warfare, how to listen to God and be sensitive to His Spirit. These sessions are open to any church members able to attend.

6 There are a number of intercession groups, some to pray for the whole of Kingdom Faith, others targeting specific areas of activity.

7 There is a group that prays particularly for Israel.

8 There are a number of individuals called to an intercessory ministry. Some pray for me in particular, and for the other leaders at Kingdom Faith.

9 There are a number of spontaneous prayer sessions before and during specific outreaches to schools and local towns. Every activity is soaked in prayer.

10 A group meets to pray during every service. There is even a prayer group praying for the prayer meeting!

11 In addition, of course, everyone has his or her own personal times of prayer.

12 And we all learn to pray without ceasing! In the midst of the daily activities of our lives.

From the above you see how essential it is to be a praying people if we are to be a revived people. It is important that we pray with faith, expecting positive answers from God. It is the faith with which we pray that matters. **If you expect results when you pray, you will pray**! It would be foolish not to. If you do not expect results, there is little point in praying!

When Kingdom Faith Church began we sensed that God wanted us to pray for a twenty-five-mile radius around Roffey Place. We needed an 'open heaven' for the gospel. For over three years we have faithfully sought to obey and have prayed for all the people and every church in this area. We have prayed for the members of parliament, local government officials, the young, the old, the sick, the addicted, the bound and afflicted. Why? Because we want to reach them all with the gospel.

You will pray for those you want to reach with the truth, for you can readily appreciate that only God can change hearts and cause people to be born again.

And we continued to pray for the anointing of God's revival power which would cause us to be more effective in reaching the world with the good news of God's Kingdom.

Of course, we did more than pray, encouraging evangelistic activity in several different ways. This produced growth by addition; revival results in growth by multiplication. If we were to believe for a church of thousands, we would need revival! After only three years we were among the largest single congregations in the country, and yet still had not experienced the full blessing of multiplication.

However, prayer was preparing the way for this. When the mustard seed came, it needed to fall in well-prepared soil so that it would immediately spring up and be fruitful.

Throughout this three-year period, we thanked the Lord for a church of thousands. We saw it with the eyes of faith and prayed it into being. We prophesied over the twenty-five-mile radius and over the nation. We confessed and prayed scriptural truths over our own lives, over the church, the area and the nation. We believed the promises of God's Word:

> The Lord will indeed give what is good, and our land will yield its harvest. (Ps. 85:12)

The more we prayed, the more convinced we became that God was going to move mightily among us, and within the whole twenty-five-mile radius. Prayer became more and more exciting.

And the people persevered. Every Sunday the worship hall would be full for the main prayer meeting. They did not flag in their zeal, for we believed the spiritual destiny of our nation lies in the hands of praying people. God's chosen way of working is in response to the prayers of His children.

I was continually thankful for the team that God had provided, especially Dan Chesney who was doing the week-by-week pastoring of the church, and Michael Barling who had taken over as the Principal of the Bible College.

Dan and I together continued to teach and encourage the whole church in prayer. We preached faith until it was pouring out of everyone's hearts. And yet still we needed to see that break-through, that final event that only the Lord could accomplish, that we knew would transform everything, taking us from the stage of steady growth into phenomenal blessing.

We needed to persevere in all that we could do; but the telling factor would be what God would do! We knew He was leading us forward step by step, not to some romantic view of revival, but to the release of His anointing of power that would make us so much more effective in everything we did in His name.

The steady growth had made us very busy. What would the multiplication of phenomenal blessing bring?

16

Worship in the Spirit

'I am going to teach you to worship in the Spirit.' Sometimes things God says to you seem almost offensive! Certainly, I was surprised by this statement.

Charismatically, our worship at Kingdom Faith would have been rated as among the best at the time the Lord said this to me. Many churches would certainly envy us for our anointed worship team, most of whom had been professional musicians. Our worship cassettes sold many thousands every year. What had we been doing all those years if not worshipping in the Spirit? It was comforting to remember that Jesus frequently made radical statements that made people stop in their tracks and completely rethink their position.

'I am going to teach you how to worship in the Spirit.' The Lord explained that our present worship had come out of the charismatic move of His Spirit. It reflected what He was doing then among His people. We had to realise He was going to move in a much more powerful way than we had previously experienced in our nation. The present forms of charismatic worship would not be able to contain what He was about to do. **Changing the worship would not produce revival, but present forms could not contain or adequately express the move of the Spirit that was coming to our nation.** He would have to do a new thing among us that would reflect the new move of the Spirit He was promising.

What were we to do? The Lord showed me that we could

not put the new on top of the old. What had begun spontaneously in the charismatic movement had become stylised. It was a fact that I could travel virtually anywhere in the world and find the same forms of worship among pentecostal and charismatic people.

The Lord showed us that if we were prepared to stop worshipping in our accustomed way, He would lead us and would show us the way forward.

I went to our worship leader, Carol, and shared what the Lord had told me. All of us find security in the known and I could tell that she was fearful of stepping out into the unknown. Tearfully she asked what we were to do. 'I don't know,' I answered honestly. However, I knew that if we were obedient in forgetting our former way of worship, the Lord would do a new thing among us.

For the next three weeks we scarcely used the musicians or sang any songs. What happened was fascinating, for the Lord showed us how we could begin to meet with Him within seconds of beginning to worship. And what developed over the following weeks and months opened up realms of worship that we had never known it was possible to experience. Interestingly, visitors from South America and other areas of the world that were experiencing revival commented that our worship resembled that of the revival churches in their own nations. Obviously we were drawing closer to our objective!

We were faced with an interesting question: 'What was the purpose of worship from God's perspective?' Christians sing their songs and hymns; they have their services. But what does God make of it all? Does He sit on His throne surveying the ecclesiastical scene listening to all these services? And if He does, what does He make of them?

His desire is to meet with His children. The purpose of worship is to draw near to Him that we might meet with Him. **He taught us that we have only truly worshipped Him when we have met with Him.**

The more we meet with Him, the more like Him we

become. He wants to reveal Himself to us, so that we know Him better. He places us in Christ and His life in us, so that we may be as He is in the world. Because we know Him we are to reveal Him to the world and declare the mighty works He performs.

Any life of faith and victory will be filled with praise, even in the most difficult circumstances. David was no stranger to adversity and often described the difficulties that confronted him, the opposition he faced and his internal conflicts. He knew, though, that no matter what the situation, his greatest need was to praise God. 'Yet will I praise you, O Lord', is typical of his attitude. He appreciated that God never changed, His Word was always true and His promises never failed, no matter what his circumstances.

The opening verses of Psalm 103 are a classic example of this. Here he speaks to himself, to his own soul. It is as if he is saying to himself: 'Take your eyes off the situation, David. Bless God and remember the great things He has done for you.'

> Praise the Lord, O my soul; all my inmost being, praise his holy name. Praise the Lord, O my soul, and forget not all his benefits – who forgives all your sins and heals all your diseases, who redeems your life from the pit and crowns you with love and compassion, who satisfies your desires with good things so that your youth is renewed like the eagle's. (Ps. 103:1–5)

The effect of doing this, or redirecting his focus, is obvious; for by the end of the Psalm he is telling the angels, the whole heavenly host and all God's obedient servants to join him in praising the Lord!

All this is in line with New Testament teaching. We are encouraged to 'rejoice in the Lord always', 'be joyful always', 'to give thanks in all circumstances', for this is God's will for us in Christ Jesus!

The devil wants Christians to analyse themselves, to focus

on themselves and their past, especially the failure and the negatives to which they have been subjected. For he knows that the more we look at ourselves, the more faith ebbs away. And he is directly opposed to God's Word which tells us to fix our eyes on Jesus, to set our hearts and minds on things above.

This does not lead us into unreality; quite the opposite. God's Word is intensely practical and tells us not only that we have the victory in Christ, but how to stand in that victory. **Whenever we focus on Jesus our hearts are immediately filled with praise for Him because He is so wonderful.**

Praise directs us to God and who He is by nature, that we may meet with Him and our lives may be impacted afresh by Him. So when we praise God we should expect to meet with Him:

> Praise the Lord, O my soul. O Lord, my God, you are very great; you are clothed with splendour and majesty. (Ps. 104:1)

We are to know Him in His glory and majesty – and this is the central theme of Psalm 145.

> I will exalt you, my God the King; I will praise your name for ever and ever. Every day I will praise you and extol your name for ever and ever. (Ps. 145:1–2)

All true praise is directed to the Lord. It declares His glory, who He is and what He has done. It is not singing about God, and it is certainly not singing about ourselves.

There is a place for singing about the life and victory we have, encouraging one another by proclaiming the truth. It is good when God's people become excited by singing of these things, and the level of faith can rise noticeably in a meeting when they do so. However, this is not strictly praise. For when we praise God, we express ourselves to

Him in worship by concentrating on who He is and what He has done. In scripture there is not a distinction between worship and praise.

We are told by Jesus that we must worship in Spirit and in truth, that all who worship God must worship in this way. In other words, all other worship is unacceptable to God. He has given us the Holy Spirit to enable us to worship in Spirit. In reality much worship is really soulish; it is aimed more at pleasing the worshipper than the Lord!

Worship in the Spirit is inspired by the Holy Spirit. He alone is to lead our worship. He alone can cause us to worship in the way that God desires so that we genuinely meet with Him. To have a sense of His presence is not necessarily to meet with Him!

Supposing the monarch or national president was present at a service. Everybody would be conscious of his presence, yet not every member of the congregation would necessarily have the privilege of meeting him by shaking his hand.

We can sense the presence of the Lord without necessarily hearing from Him or having a real encounter with Him; He is more than a feeling!

When we sense His presence this should encourage us to move on in our worship so that we do meet with Him. How frustrating to leave the meeting place at the end of a service, knowing that you have not met with the Lord. You may be able to say that it was a good meeting, the Lord was present, the preaching anointed, and yet still not really be touched or moved by God in your spirit.

All the heavenly host are spiritual beings because flesh and blood cannot inherit God's Kingdom. In the book of Revelation we are given a wonderful insight into the worship in heaven. If anybody knows how to worship in the Spirit, therefore, it must be the heavenly host! Those nearest the throne are the four living creatures:

> Day and night they never stop saying: 'Holy, holy, holy is the Lord God Almighty, who was, and is, and is to come.' (Rev. 4:8)

Notice the strength and power of these words. It is clear from scripture that **the Lord is 'majestic in holiness, awesome in glory, working wonders'** (Exod. 15:11). The Holy One is the King, the Lord of Glory. And the Glorious One is Holy. All the praise in heaven seems to have the note of strength and power. It is strong, not weak, insipid or dreamy!

The living creatures are described as giving 'glory, honour and thanks to him who sits on the throne and who lives for ever and ever' (Rev. 4:9). This is what we are to do when we worship the Lord. As the creatures praise God, the twenty-four elders 'worship him'. How? They declare who He is and how worthy He is:

> You are worthy, our Lord and God, to receive glory and honour and power, for you created all things, and by your will they were created and have their being. (Rev. 4:11)

They worship by praising God for who He is and what He has done. They do not sit or stand around saying how wonderful and privileged they are to be elders and what good feelings they have for the Lord. Their whole focus is on Him! This is also the case with the angelic host:

> Then I looked and heard the voice of many angels, numbering thousands upon thousands, and ten thousand times ten thousand. They encircled the throne and the living creatures and the elders. In a loud voice they sang: 'Worthy is the Lamb, who was slain, to receive power and wealth and wisdom and strength and honour and glory and praise!' (Rev. 5:11–12)

Notice they all sing *loudly*, each of these millions of angels. Heaven is a noisy place. I feel for those who think they are going there for some peace and quiet; they will feel completely out of place! Heaven is noisy and full of activity. What about those who say: 'I don't like all this praise'? They had better have a change of heart for, if they are born again, they will be praising God in heaven for all eternity. And such praise will not be confined to heaven.

> Then I heard every creature in heaven and on earth and under the earth and on the sea, and all that is in them, singing: 'To him who sits on the throne and to the Lamb be praise and honour and glory and power, for ever and ever!' (Rev. 5:13)

Wherever there is genuine praise it is centred on the Father and His Son – the Lamb, Jesus. And all in the power of the Spirit.

Because you have been redeemed you are mentioned in chapter 7:

> After this I looked and there before me was a great multitude that no one could count, from every nation, tribe, people and language, standing before the throne and in front of the Lamb . . . And they cried out in a loud voice: 'Salvation belongs to our God, who sits on the throne, and to the Lamb.' (Rev. 7:9–10)

All who praise are focused on the throne, not on themselves. They are not saying 'how wonderful that we have been saved'; they are proclaiming the praise of the One who gives salvation. They fall before the throne in worship saying:

> Amen! Praise and glory and wisdom and thanks and honour and power and strength be to our God for ever and ever. Amen! (Rev. 7:12)

All this gives us a wonderful insight as to how we can stand before the throne and praise God, meeting with Him when we worship *now*. When we praise Him here on earth we are joining in with the continuous activity of worship in heaven.

How can God receive power and wealth and wisdom and strength? Surely He is the One who possesses all these things. How can we, and the heavenly host, give them to Him?

In and of ourselves this would be impossible. However, we are in Christ and His Spirit is within us. We can therefore worship with all the riches and resources God has made available to us in the Spirit. If we are to worship with all power, to express our love for Him with all our strength, then there will be nothing half-hearted about the way we praise God. No wonder the heavenly host sing and speak with loud voices; for they are praising the Lord with all their might.

And this is exactly what David was encouraging himself to do, to praise with his whole being.

Now from these scriptures in Revelation we can glean a number of characteristics about worship in the Spirit.

1. **The place of worship is around the throne**. Jesus has made it possible for us to approach the throne of grace.
2. **All the praise is directed to the Lord**. We can sing spiritual songs to one another, but when we worship our praise is to be directed to Him.
3. **Praise proclaims who God is**: Holy, Almighty, Eternal, Lord.
4. **Praise declares that God is worthy** to receive from all He has created in heaven and on earth, glory, honour, power, wealth, wisdom and strength. You can only give to God in this way because you are in Christ and His Spirit is in you.
5. **Praise is not singing about yourself**, but about the Lord and what He has done.

All this is a far cry from what passes as worship in some places. In some liturgical services it is difficult to come before the throne and encounter God because the people are given little time or opportunity to do so. There is little or no sense of passing into the Holy of Holies with sincere hearts and in full assurance of faith, expecting to encounter the Lord.

Even in many pentecostal or charismatic circles the results are not much better. At the beginning of the service people go through the routine of singing a few songs, some to God, some to one another, others about themselves, again with little sense of coming before God's throne and actually meeting with Him. The people are usually dependent on being led by men, by the pastor, the worship leader and musicians. There is little sense of entering into a personal encounter with God.

This is not an attempt to be critical, but simply to describe the situation that often exists. Many pastors and worship leaders have told me they have been stuck in a rut with their worship; they have sensed that God wanted to change things, but have been at a loss as to what to do.

Certainly, from the platform it is apparent that many people come into services ill-prepared for worship. For the first two or three songs several will not be singing at all, others will be looking around (to see who is there or what they are wearing?), while others appear to be mindlessly reading the words from a screen or songsheet. Few appear to be meeting with God.

The worship leader will often exhort and encourage everybody to participate and 'really praise God'. Gradually people become involved and just as the worship is beginning to be filled with God's presence, it is time to stop and move on to the next part of the service! There may be some singing in the Spirit first, but this is likely to last only a minute or two.

The worship of most pentecostal and charismatic churches came out of the move of God that took place in the seventies. At first there was a freshness and spontaneity in the praise. The songs were often extremely simple, but they were sung with anointing. As often happens with a move of God, slowly man begins to organise what the Spirit began. The songs become more complicated, the musical groups more professional (but not necessarily more anointed!) and the leader takes greater control and direction of the meeting. Slowly but surely man has taken over from the Spirit, instead of being led by the Spirit. It has become a form.

Some churches are now experiencing fresh anointing from the Holy Spirit and this is beginning to affect the worship, which is such an important aspect of any church's corporate activity. **A life of faith and victory will be full of praise for God.** And His power should be released among those who truly worship in Spirit and truth.

You have received the Holy Spirit and He never runs out of inspiration. God would not tell you that you must worship in Spirit and truth without giving you the resources to do so. Whenever you worship you should expect to meet with God, not simply sing words to Him; to know that He is truly imparting His life afresh to you because He is so great:

> Great is the Lord and most worthy of praise; his greatness no one can fathom. (Ps. 145:3)

You will not know His greatness by simply thinking about Him; only by encountering Him in His majestic holiness and glory!

> One generation will commend your works to another; they will tell of your mighty acts. They will speak of the glorious splendour of your majesty, and I will meditate on your wonderful works. (Ps. 145:4–5)

You are to speak of the glorious splendour of God's majesty. However, you can only speak of what you know. You can meditate on His wonderful works, but to be able to speak of Him as He is, you need to know Him as He is. You can only be an instrument of revelation to others when you know the One of whom you speak.

And it is clear that you are not to speak only of His mercy, His grace, His love, but also of His majesty.

> All you have made will praise you, O Lord; your saints will extol you. They will tell of the glory of your kingdom and speak of your might, so that all men may know of your mighty acts and the glorious splendour of your kingdom. (Ps. 145:10–12)

As one who is in Christ, you are one of those saints. **Clearly it is God's purpose for you to know the glorious splendour of His majesty and Kingdom, or He would not expect you to speak of these things.** This is to be your present witness, not what you will do when you go to heaven! It will be too late then to tell others of these things. God wants 'all men' to hear of these wonderful truths.

'My mouth will speak in praise of the Lord,' (v. 21) says David. This praise language is not to be confined to the worship meeting or our prayer times. No, we are to be speaking His praises continually. This comes from an attitude of heart. If praise for Him is in your heart you will not be able to keep quiet. 'For out of the overflow of the heart the mouth speaks' (Matt. 12:34).

The devil wants you to believe that it is impossible for you to know God in such a glorious way. He wants to try and prevent you from enjoying this wonderful privilege. Remember, he once knew that glory, but was thrown out of heaven when he rebelled against the Lord! The blood of Jesus makes it possible for you to enter into that place which is for ever denied to Satan. How can you do this?

Here is a simple way. Do not treat the following as a method but as an expression of your heart. If your worship is to be real it has to come from the heart; it is your true expression of love and praise to God. You are not, therefore, dependent upon a worship leader, musicians, or even songs to praise God, although all these have their place. The worship comes from your heart, is inspired by the Holy Spirit and is in no way dependent on man.

1. **Open your heart to God.** Speak to Him and tell Him what is on your heart – not what should be, but what is there. Do not say to God what you think He wants to hear. You are not performing for Him; you need to be real and honest.
2. As you do this, **speak words to Him.** Actually express these on your lips. This can be done softly by a whole congregation without people speaking so loudly that their neighbours can hear what is being said.
3. **If there is any sin to be confessed, bring it to the Lord for His forgiveness.** Remember He cleanses you immediately.
4. **Forgive any who need your forgiveness**. You want nothing to hinder your relationship with God in worship.
5. **Cast any burdens on the Lord**. You do this very briefly by handing them over to Him. He will take care of them. You do not want your worship time to be full of worrying about your problems. It is to be full of Jesus; then He will take care of the needs.
6. **All the above need take only two or three minutes** when you are used to worshipping God heart to heart.
7. **Begin to thank the Lord for His forgiveness, His mercy, grace and love; for blessings received, for His faithfulness, for whatever is on your heart**. You are entering through the gate of thanksgiving into the courts of praise.
8. **Speak more loudly as you do this**. Even when you are on your own it is good to thank and praise aloud if possible. In a congregational setting everybody is now thanking God aloud at the same time. Yet He is able to hear the expression of every heart. We are not at the worship meeting to listen to one another, but to meet with God.
9. **All the above needs to be in our own language**. Do not hide behind speaking in tongues. When you use this gift your mind is unfruitful. You need to engage your heart and mind with God.
10. **Your thanksgiving will soon become praise for God**; the one will lead into the other. And the volume will increase

still more, for as with the heavenly host, you are to praise God with a loud voice, whether you are on your own or within a congregational setting. It is liberating to praise God in this way. It is only the flesh that wants to praise in a subdued way, or not at all! Self-consciousness is sin, a work of the flesh! Press on through this flesh barrier. You are to meet with God, not be restricted by your flesh which opposes the work of God's Spirit in you.

11 As you begin to praise, you will soon exhaust your vocabulary, and will need to begin speaking in tongues. Do not confine this to one or two minutes. **Be prepared to pray in the Spirit either by speaking or singing, for several minutes**.

12 **Flow from tongues to your own language, then back to tongues, then back to your own language, and so on**. In this way you will keep both your spirit and mind involved in what you are doing. You will maintain your concentration. It is possible to speak in tongues without concentrating fully on what you are doing. By flowing from tongues to your own language alternately you remain fully involved and you begin to see the direction in which the Holy Spirit is leading your worship. He who speaks in a tongue should also pray for the interpretation.

13 **Worship in the Spirit will never be boring, neither will it be repetitive**. He will lead you in a different way on every occasion. He will never run out of inspiration, for He is God.

14 **Sometimes you may be in the high praises of God**. It is as if you are with the whole host of heaven proclaiming the greatness and worthiness of our God. **At other times you may be reduced to silence by the awesome sense of His presence**; not an awkward silence where nothing is happening, but one in which you know He is speaking to you.

I repeat, you can praise like this on your own or within a congregational context. In a public service it is good for the musicians to play their instruments in the Spirit when the people begin to sing in the Spirit. **They are there to accompany the people in worship, not dominate or take over**. At some point the leader can sensitively lead into an appropriate song, expressing praise for God. Everything, remember, is to be focused on the Lord. Attention should not be drawn back to the worship leader, neither is this an appropriate time for solos! The leader should not interrupt the flow of the Spirit with his own anecdotes or pieces of teaching. He should be as inconspicuous as possible, so that everybody's concentration can be fully on the Lord. **All the people praising God all the time**!

If the singing in the Spirit is allowed to go on for several minutes, interspersed with the occasional praise song, most people will meet with God.

Not only do we worship in this way in Kingdom Faith Church, but I have introduced others in many nations to this way of flowing with the Holy Spirit in worship, allowing Him to be in control and to lead. He will come upon people in fresh anointing and blessing. Many come to a new place with the Lord in such times of worship. They encounter Him for the first time in His majesty and glory and receive great blessing. Some are filled with the Holy Spirit as they worship, others are healed by God as they meet with Him.

This is not the reason for worshipping in this way, however. **We are meeting to worship the Lord for Himself, to seek Him for who He is**, not because of what we want to receive from Him. We meet to bless Him, to express our love for Him.

However, when you give, you receive. **You can never outdo the Lord in giving! When you give of yourself, He gives of Himself; for with the measure used it will be measured to you. You reap what you sow!** When you give to Him He gives back to you His good measure, pressed down, shaken together and running over.

What a wonderful God! So full of love that He draws you to Himself! You are not seeking to enter a place where He does not want you, or where you do not belong. No, you are coming into the place He appointed for you when Jesus died on the cross.

The veil of the temple was torn apart, opening the way for *all* believers to enter the Holy of Holies, to come before the throne of God and meet with Him in His glory! Then they can go from His presence and tell all men of 'the glorious splendour of His majesty and speak of His mighty acts'.

God indeed takes us from mercy to majesty. Because of His great and wonderful mercy, you can know Him in His majesty now, you can reign in life and eternally with Him in glory.

There is no way that I can adequately express how we have been blessed through allowing the Lord to take us into fresh dimensions of revival worship. To be among a people who consistently meet with God in this way is a great privilege. Not that we always keep to the above pattern. That is simply expressing the principles God taught us when moving us into revival worship.

I must admit it is difficult when I travel to be back in the realms of man-dominated worship. However, in general people have been so responsive when led into a greater freedom in worship, learning to flow with the Spirit and to hand the leadership over to Him! And it has been wonderful to see how people have met with God as a result.

I believe it will not be long before such worship becomes commonplace, because it will express the stronger move of the Spirit that people will experience in revival.

17

The Joy of the Lord

There is nothing new in people being liberated in joy by the Holy Spirit. Recently many in different nations have experienced a refreshing of the Spirit, which some were calling revival. Others were confused by the whole experience, wondering even whether it was truly of God. Their doubts were understandable in the light of the amazing scenes of apparent disorder wherever this joy broke out. Tales of preachers being unable to preach, leaders stating that they had no need to bother about the Word because the Spirit would move anyway, understandably raised further doubts. The fact that for several months some churches were having one meeting after another where people were given the impression that only if they were laughing were they really released in God, also caused consternation. For some, what had begun as a refreshing from God was becoming boring as they were being subjected to the same diet over and over again.

And yet from the testimonies of changed lives, release from bondages and healings received, there could be little doubt that a real work of God was taking place in many people.

Some complained that fleshly manifestations were taking place; and they were no doubt correct in this assessment. But what move of God has not produced accompanying fleshly manifestations? After all, God is working out His purposes in human nature. Receiving an anointing does not immediately make a person perfect. Besides, resisting what the Holy Spirit is doing is certainly more fleshly than some people getting carried away with an excess of joy! And if people are 'drunk in the Spirit', they will appear drunk!

This was the experience when God first poured out the Holy Spirit on believers at Pentecost. The Holy Spirit came upon them as a mighty wind and flames of fire, and they spoke in other tongues. The impact of what was happening drove the 120 who were present out of the room where they were meeting and into the streets. There a great cosmopolitan crowd gathered. Those who were newly filled with the Holy Spirit were behaving in such strange ways that some bystanders made fun of them and said, 'They have had too much wine' (Acts 2:13).

They appeared to be drunk because they were behaving as drunken people do. However, the scripture continues: 'Then Peter stood up with the Eleven, raised his voice and addressed the crowd . . .' (v. 14).

Now if he stood up, presumably Peter was on the ground. Perhaps he appeared drunk like the others, or was simply overcome by the Spirit. However, he was immediately sober when he needed to preach the Word; and it seems he preached uninterrupted by the events around him.

He explained that these scenes of 'drunkenness' were the fulfilment of what God had promised. He quoted from the prophecy of Joel, and said in effect: 'This is what we have been waiting for during these past hundreds of years.' Even though the Lord had promised His people that 'their hearts will be glad as with wine' (Zech. 10:7), the people did not expect such scenes to accompany the outpouring of God's Spirit.

The anointing the disciples received in Jerusalem thrust them out into the streets of the city in evangelism. Three thousand came to the Lord that day. **The anointing they received was obviously more than a release of joy, but also included the seed of miraculous multiplication.** This is confirmed by events recorded in the ensuing chapters of Acts as the Church grew greatly in numbers and at a very fast rate.

So there was joy and drunkenness when the Spirit came, **but there was more!**

I came to see that the joy was the subjective side of receiving the Spirit and brought wonderful blessing and release to many. But several churches that were enjoying this refreshing were not seeing mighty multiplication because an essential element in the anointing God wanted His people to receive was missing.

This is not to deny the value of the joy, or the subjective experience. How can we 'rejoice in the Lord always' without having a release of joy in our lives? As I travelled in different parts of the world, I was disturbed by the number of churches that seemed to have no direction as a result of receiving this time of refreshing. The Holy Spirit is given to lead us – and He does not take us in circles going over the same ground again and again.

It seemed that many churches did not know how to build around the anointing or to turn it into evangelistic fruitfulness that would make them more successful in reaching the world with the gospel, which is the objective of revival. It was not until I received the 'mustard seed anointing' that I appreciated what exactly was lacking.

Kingdom Faith Church, together with many other churches in Britain, certainly experienced the release of joy and there is no doubt that this was a great blessing to many. Some people experienced considerable personal release and change in their lives.

I was keen that this should only become a general experience at Kingdom Faith in God's way and in His timing. If this was to be part of His build-up towards the revival we were seeking, He would initiate events in the right way and at the right time.

Some months previously while I was getting ready for bed one night, suddenly without any warning the Holy Spirit came upon me and I laughed and laughed and laughed. It was as well that my wife was the only witness of this event, as I was rolling about on the bed in uncontrollable joy!

After some time it seemed safe to go to bed; but no sooner was I under the duvet than the laughter broke out again. The noise kept everyone in the household awake, and we ended by having a prayer meeting on the landing in the early hours of the morning.

As soon as this blessing came to us all at Kingdom Faith, I was immediately saying to the Lord: 'What's next?' I was determined that we were not going to become stuck in a kind of spiritual cul-de-sac, having one laughter meeting after another, and so lose our impetus of moving towards revival.

This blessing was like a fresh baptism in the Holy Spirit and had spread very rapidly in Britain, but mainly among pentecostal and charismatic churches where people had previous experience of the Holy Spirit.

Jesus promised the disciples power when the Holy Spirit came upon them. I knew the Lord was telling me that after the joy would come the power, that **He was leading us not only to a release of joy but a release of power beyond anything we had known previously**. First, however, we would have some weeks to enjoy the joy! During this time we saw as never before how much there is about the Lord's joy in scripture.

Jesus was certainly the most joyful man ever to have lived. When speaking of His own Son, God says:

> You have loved righteousness and hated wickedness; therefore God, your God, has set you above your companions by anointing you with the oil of joy. (Heb. 1:9)

It was joy that marked Jesus off from all those around Him, even though there is no evidence that He was ever 'drunk' in the Spirit.

For years I had spoken of joy as being the barometer of our faith. As soon as we stop rejoicing in the Lord we have ceased to believe that God is bigger than our circumstances. To concentrate on yourself, your circumstances and problems is enough to make anyone lose his or her joy! **To concentrate on the Lord, and to rejoice in Him, is to place Him higher than the problems and is evidence of our trust in Him.**

At one pastors' conference at Roffey Place, there was a tremendous release of joy, and many of the leaders were released from years of feeling burdened by their problems and responsibilities. After the conference we received many testimonies of changed lives and ministries. Of course, the joy was simply the outward expression of a release of the Holy Spirit that was taking place in people. The practical effects of this release varied from one person to another. Before the joy there were tears for some.

For several months I was being used by the Lord to bring this blessing into several strategic churches overseas. On one occasion there was a great release of joy among the people and many were drunk in the Spirit, when He suddenly said to me, 'I now want to move in an entirely different way. I want to bless my people with peace.' I looked at the scenes around me and thought, 'Only God can bring peace into such a situation.' Nearly everyone was laughing uncontrollably at the time, drunk with the Spirit of God.

The Holy Spirit wants to keep complete control in meetings. As I called for order through the microphone, everybody immediately became quiet. The sudden transformation that took place was awesome. A supernatural peace descended on the whole congregation and the Lord then graciously began to heal people.

In the first chapter of this book I spoke of the first three evenings of the conference at which the Lord used Hector Gimenèz to minister anointing to me. On the first evening there was a great release of joy, with many hundreds drunk in the Spirit, the pastor and his wife in particular! Yet on the second evening I knew the Lord wanted to do something completely different. He did not want a repetition of the first evening. And on the third and subsequent evenings He moved yet again in entirely different ways. Such is the variety of the Holy Spirit.

Together with all at Kingdom Faith, I was grateful to the Lord for the positive blessings brought through this particular release of the Holy Spirit. But I was hungry for a move of God that would produce a spiritual awakening in our nation; it would not be changed by Christians rolling around on the floor laughing, enjoyable as that might be. No, we would need to see the release of His power in our lives. Like the first believers we would need an anointing that motivated us for evangelism and enabled us to be abundantly fruitful in it. It is great to rejoice, but we want to see nations saved!

I could not escape the fact that the Church in our country had enjoyed twenty-five years of charismatic blessing, during which time the nation deteriorated seriously in its social, moral and spiritual values. We could not afford another move that blessed the Church, but did not reach the nation.

It was wonderful to be refreshed by the Lord, but we needed the anointing that would enable us to bless others, not only to receive blessing for ourselves. **We must have a much more powerful move of God to bless the nation and bring salvation to millions! We must have revival!**

18

The Bright Light

After praying for me, Hector Gimènez saw a bright shaft of light shining from heaven on to me. This reflected back on to him and he received a fresh anointing. Then it overflowed to all the people at the meeting.

For a few weeks after receiving the anointing for multiplication I didn't think anything further about this. I had not seen this light myself, although I was deeply conscious of the Lord's presence at the time. To me it seemed part of the total event that was awesome, yet seemingly of no greater significance than to be part of the way in which the Lord had chosen to work.

It was while preparing for the final meeting of our Revival Conference, held a few weeks later, that God spoke to me about this light. He reminded me that He never did anything without purpose and that every way in which His Spirit moves reveals truth from scripture.

We had been seeking God for revival, for the anointing that would be a blessing for our nation as well as for our church. The Kingdom of God needed to be extended in our land and beyond. The kingdom of darkness therefore needed to retreat before the Light of Jesus Christ. He is the Light of the World and the darkness cannot overcome Him.

I sensed the Lord was directing me to Isaiah, chapter 9, and from this scripture He spoke to me about why that bright light had shone from heaven.

> The people walking in darkness have seen a great light; on those living in the land of the shadow of death a light has dawned. (Isa. 9:2)

A great light! That is what Hector had seen! Certainly in the days following the anointing, I experienced the Holy Spirit coming upon me again and again. Sometimes this was quite disarming as it seemed He was exposing areas of darkness in me that needed to be cleansed. The light was not only shining on me but shining within me.

And the anointing that this light brought overflowed on to others! Many at Kingdom Faith had also experienced God dealing with unresolved issues in their lives. The Lord was cleansing the temple so that His light could shine more effectively out of us. Did not Jesus say that our light is to shine before men?

The next verse in Isaiah 9 speaks of the effect of this bright light: 'You have multiplied the nation', verse 3 reads in the New King James Version that I was using at the time. This was the anointing of multiplication with which God would bless our nation.

> You have enlarged the nation and increased their joy; they rejoice before you as people rejoice at the harvest, as men rejoice when dividing the plunder. (Isa. 9:3)

This was amazing. Already at Kingdom Faith we were rejoicing 'as people rejoice at the harvest'. Not only did we believe that God could cause the congregation to become a church of thousands, we somehow knew this would happen. The church was in a new place of faith, believing what we could not see. In our spirits we could see the great harvest of souls, the church of thousands, tens of thousands even.

What had appeared as a good faith goal no longer seemed a distant possibility but something that was inevitable. Only God could have worked such a change in people's hearts!

When a farmer sows seed, he waits for the green shoots

to burst through the surface. When he looks at the field, he sees not only small shoots, but the harvest that will inevitably result. He can see in his mind's eye the golden grain. The green shoots are simply the first evidence of what will follow.

A casual spectator might only see green shoots without having any vision for what will follow. He has not sown the seed and has no expectation of harvest.

At Kingdom Faith there was great joy at the prospect of what was going to develop out of the revival that had now begun And what follows in Isaiah 9 excited us greatly.

Through the three-year history of Kingdom Faith Church we had often spoken of the fact that it is the anointing that breaks the yoke of oppression. We had been seeking the anointing to break the yoke not only over our area, but over the nation. Not that such an anointing would be confined to one ministry, but we were conscious of our calling to be the tip of the arrow and so we needed to keep looking to the Lord for such an anointing.

> You have shattered the yoke that burdens them, the bar across their shoulders, the rod of their oppressor. (Isa. 9:4)

I suddenly realised that the anointing of multiplication we had received would not only lead to fast growth of our church, but that the miraculous, abundant harvest was possible because this was also the anointing that shatters the yoke that has burdened God's people.

The Hebrew word means to shatter into tiny pieces. The yoke would be irreplaceable! And the rod of the oppressor was also shattered. Satan had used that rod to inflict sickness, oppression and defeat on many Christians. Now we had the anointing that shattered that rod into tiny pieces.

I was so excited as I went to the revival meeting to share this revelation with everyone. We had removed most of the chairs from our worship centre to cram in as many people as possible. There was a great release of faith as I preached from Isaiah 9, and then the Spirit of God moved really powerfully.

Somehow this was different from any other occasion of spiritual warfare. Together we proclaimed victory over the enemy. It was obvious that many were being freed from oppression and sickness in a variety of forms. Then several people received an anointing from God to exercise particular ministries of healing.

Now that we had experienced the break-through into revival our meetings seemed so much more powerful. And there was such a sense of God's victory over our lives and the church. We knew that we could go out with this anointing and see God's victory over the enemy wherever we went.

19

Faith For Revival

There are so many aspects of God's nature and character that we have not been able to include within this small book. He never changes, although our perception of Him often does. He encourages you in love; at times He disciplines you in love. Yet He *always* loves you.

He is *always* merciful towards you. There are several ways in which you will experience His mercy: in forgiveness, as He patiently teaches you, in His provision and healing. **He is always merciful because it is His nature to be so**.

And yet while He is dispensing mercy to one, He can bring swift judgement to another at precisely the same time, especially to any opposing Him. He deals personally with each individual at any given moment. It is impossible for us to understand how He can do this. He is God, and so is far greater than we could ever know.

To live in faith is to live in the daily knowledge of God's mercy and forgiveness. He does not judge you. He does not survey your life looking for faults. He has placed you in His Son and He sees you wearing His righteousness and holiness.

To live in faith is to be dependent on His grace, receiving one blessing after another. You know that you can do nothing of yourself, and so you trust Him to give freely of Himself to supply your every need.

To live in faith, therefore, is to live in dependence on the life and resources of God's Holy Spirit within you. You live in Jesus and His Spirit lives in you. His person is within you. Therefore you lack no good thing. You stand complete in Him.

To live in faith is to live in continual praise of the One who has called and chosen you. His praise is continually on your lips. You rejoice in Him, for no matter what your situation, He never changes. His life is your life. He withholds nothing of Himself from you and lives to reveal Himself to you.

To live in faith is, therefore, to live in joy, a joy that is not dependent on circumstances, but which comes from your knowledge of Him, rejoicing that He is both with you always and living in you. Your joy in Jesus will carry you through every situation.

To live in faith is to live in God's Word, therefore. For although situations change, His Word never does. It is eternal truth. He watches over His Word to perform it. Although there will be many occasions when you will be tempted to believe your feelings instead of His Word, you learn this is never the path of victory. For your victory is dependent on holding fast to the Word in the face of everything that is contrary. For circumstances will never change God's Word; but faith in God's Word will change your circumstances.

To live in faith is to live in peace. He is your peace and He is with you always to impart that peace to you. When you fail or sin, His mercy restores your peace. When you feel you are struggling and you count Jesus as your Victor, you are immediately at peace about the situation, even if no immediate change is apparent.

To live in faith is to live in love, for all that counts is faith working through love.

To live in faith is to live in victory; because that victory belongs to the Lord. You are in Him, and He has given you victory in our Lord Jesus Christ.

To live in faith is to live in the knowledge of your salvation, that you are totally and eternally made acceptable to God because you live in the One who is always acceptable to Him. You are never outside of that acceptance or of the covenant of love in which He has placed you. Even when you fail to keep your side of the covenant agreement, He will never be faithless; He will never fail to keep His Word to you.

It is only a few weeks since God imparted the anointing of multiplication to us at Kingdom Faith and yet already we are enjoying the first-fruits of this great blessing. No longer do we have to say that He is leading us towards revival; now we are enjoying this wonderful privilege.

It would be true to say that to us it seems that everything has changed in these last few weeks. There is an even greater release of God's Spirit in our worship. Many lives are being changed as this seed takes root and begins to produce further evidence of Kingdom Life within people.

But the most significant fruit is that already we are seeing multiplication. The growth rate of the church has multiplied four-fold already. The number of healings has increased.

One testimony of many will give the flavour of what is happening. A teenage girl who had only been a Christian for a few weeks was told by her doctor that she had cervical cancer. He had the X-ray proof for this. Undaunted, the girl immediately told him that on the following Friday she would go to the youth meeting and ask for prayer, and stated that she knew the Lord would heal her. She asked for an appointment for the following week so that she could have a further X-ray that would demonstrate she had been healed.

On the Friday she was prayed for, returned to the doctor on the following Monday and was X-rayed. On the Wednesday she returned for the result of this examination and was told that all traces of the cervical cancer had disappeared. She asked for copies of the X-rays both before and after her healing.

This is the boldness of faith in a new believer of only six weeks. Not only are more people coming to the Lord, but the level of commitment and faith they are demonstrating from the very beginning of their Christian lives is so encouraging.

Because of the rapid growth of the church, we have had a problem of space for over eighteen months, needing two, then three, then four services to accommodate everybody. The Lord gave us vision to build a National Revival Centre, a large auditorium with the necessary facilities to host conferences to which people can come from across the nation and beyond. There they will meet with God in revival power, receive the anointing of multiplication and take that blessing back to their own churches.

As I write this, the National Revival Centre, which can seat almost 2,000, is nearing completion. Kingdom Faith Church will meet in this building, of course, but at the present rate of growth it will not be long before that is filled and we will need to have multiple services again.

Already pastors, leaders and other believers are coming from all over the nation, and from many other countries too, to receive the anointing of multiplication because they have heard of the things that are taking place here. Every month there are conferences on various aspects of revival, teaching people how to apply the anointing of the Holy Spirit to various aspects of Body life so that the anointing bears abundant fruitfulness.

For three years we have moved towards this point. All the hours of prayer, of seeking God have proved worth while. The arrow has broken through in revival. This is totally the work of God's grace. Now others can follow without having to go through the same three-year process. We are happy about that, for our purpose has been to be true to God's call, to see His Kingdom come and His will done in our nation and beyond.

As a ministry and church we want to continue to be available to help and encourage others; to share the anointing of multiplication.

The words spoken over me when I received this anointing shall be fulfilled: 'You are going to travel through the world and you are going to impart this anointing to many.'

All the praise and glory belongs to our God: the Lord of

mercy, grace and love; the God of majesty. May He lead you from mercy to majesty! May you receive this impartation from the Lord. I pray that when you do, it will be seed falling in good soil that will produce thirty, sixty or a hundred times what was sown.